right to their exclusive claim, Jesus has not only fulfilled the law but also abolished it, and the Gentile nations henceforth will share in God's redemption. Luke also lays stress on the universality of the good tidings by showing how they were carried specifically to the poor and underprivileged. Finally, John, writing from a different point of view and with a different purpose, emphasizes the unity of God's new people.

Laymen will welcome a book that presents the beginnings of the faith in a manner at once so scholarly and so readable.

The Author

Howard Clark Kee, an ordained Methodist minister, earned his doctorate at Yale University after special study at the American School of Oriental Research in Jerusalem and Jordan. He then became Instructor in Religious Thought at the University of Pennsylvania, remaining in this capacity from 1951 to 1953. Since 1953, Dr. Kee has been on the faculty of the Theological School of Drew University, Madison, New Jersey, where he is now Associate Professor of New Testament. He is the author of *Making Ethical Decisions* in the Layman's Theological Library.

JESUS AND GOD'S NEW PEOPLE

The Four Gospels

WESTMINSTER GUIDES TO THE BIBLE

Edwin M. Good, General Editor

JESUS
AND GOD'S
NEW PEOPLE

The Four Gospels

by

HOWARD CLARK KEE

Philadelphia
THE WESTMINSTER PRESS

LIBRARY OF CONGRESS CATALOG CARD NO. 59-9522

Contents

Preface

If we did not have the four Gospels, we would have no information about Jesus. But why are there *four* of them? Why is there not only one? Why are there significant differences among the four? Such questions as these indicate that the Gospels do not exist solely to give information. As a matter of fact, this book suggests that the more important purpose of the Gospels is to present a point of view — the point of view, not of four biographers, but of four men who reflect profoundly the faith of the Christian church.

That faith, indeed, provides the key with which this book seeks to unlock the riches of the four Gospels. Without avoiding or minimizing problems and difficulties, the author steers his course straight to the heart of the matter. And he finds the heart of the matter to be in the staggering affirmation of the Christian gospel: that in Jesus Christ we meet God at work for our reconciliation. This faith informs every passage of the Gospels, and the way in which the varying kinds of expression point unfalteringly to the faith will open new vistas of understanding to every thoughtful reader. Too much writing on the Gospels is the product of wishful thinking. Here, the reader may be assured, is thinking that is not wishful but hopeful, which sees and draws out from the Gospels the faith that is everywhere expressed there.

The Westminster Guides to the Bible grew in the first instance out of the stimulus of the Layman's Theological Library. If, we thought, laymen in the church could be so eloquently encouraged to be theologians, why could they not be encouraged to be Biblical scholars as well? In the modern resurgence of serious thinking about the Christian faith, the study of the Bible has played a major role. But the methods and results of this recent study have not been made available to laymen.

The Westminster Guides to the Bible seek to fill this gap. In nine brief volumes, we introduce the riches of the major portions of the Bible and of the period " between the Testaments." The writers share the conviction that the Bible lies at the heart of Christianity, and that it is imperative that laymen be aided to take a firm grip on Biblical faith. We are certain that this means no denial of the mind. On the contrary, the Bible demands the utmost our minds can give it, and searching study repays our efforts with new insights.

Of course, we are primarily concerned with the Bible, not with our books about it. We hope that the reader will have his Bible in hand as he reads these books, and that he will turn to it again when he has finished. We dare to hope that he will turn from these guides with greater anticipation to the Bible itself.

And it is with laymen, who are the backbone of the church, that we are concerned. We have written, not for scholars already learned, but for those who seek to learn. We are certain that no wishy-washy faith, no cheap " religiousness," is wanted. In the vigor of Biblical faith we trust that the reader will find invigoration. If so, the church of Christ will be served.

Edwin M. Good

CHAPTER 1 | *Faith and Facts in the Gospels*

Nᴇᴀʀʟʏ forty years before the First Gospel was written down, there was a gospel. The gospel (the word means " good news ") was being preached long before anyone ever thought of producing a written account of the ministry and message of Jesus, such as the Gospel of Mark or the Gospel of John. The four Gospels are the result of the reflection on the meaning of Jesus Christ that continued for a generation or more, but the gospel was there from the very beginning of Christianity.

Tʜᴇ Bᴇɢɪɴɴɪɴɢ ᴏғ ᴛʜᴇ Gᴏsᴘᴇʟ

The gospel began when Jesus announced that " the kingdom of God is at hand," and summoned men to " repent, and believe in the gospel " (Mark 1:15). But what was involved in the good news became apparent only as Jesus' ministry continued through his words and deeds, and the meaning of the gospel was fully disclosed through his death and resurrection. The gospel Jesus preached was " the beginning of the gospel " (Mark 1:1), but it was only the beginning! The gospel that lies behind our Gospels is a response in faith to the total impact of Jesus Christ: his life, his ministry, his teachings, his crucifixion, and his encounter with his followers after God raised him from the dead. If this gospel had not exercised its trans-

9

forming power in the early church, there would have been no
Gospels. The Gospels, therefore, are neither objective historical
biographies prepared by detached observers nor theological
speculations spun out of thin air; they are responses to the
historical life, tragic death, and triumphant resurrection of
Jesus Christ.

A common core of conviction lay behind the early Christian preaching despite the differences in background, in ter-
minology, and in emphasis of the individual preachers. Theologians call the common affirmations of the first Christians the
" kerygma," which is taken directly from a Greek word meaning " proclamation." Kerygma can mean the " act of proclaiming or announcing." But, more significantly, it often means the
content of what is proclaimed, as in I Cor. 1:21: " It pleased
God through the folly of *what we preach* [Greek, *kērygma*]
to save those who believe." The forms in which the apostles
bear witness to the meaning of Christ are so varied that some
scholars insist that it is inaccurate to speak of only one
kerygma. But a unity of affirmation underlies the various ways
in which the first Christians testified to God's revelation in
Jesus of Nazareth.

A sermon attributed to Peter in Acts 10:34-43 gives a good
outline of the kerygma. It makes these points:
1. The word of Jesus Christ is the good news.
2. Jesus was anointed by God with the Holy Spirit.
3. He engaged in a healing ministry.
4. He was put to death by the Jews.
5. God raised him on the third day.
6. Witnesses were with him after the resurrection.
7. The church is commanded to preach.
8. Belief in him brings forgiveness of sins.

Although other parts of the New Testament place more emphasis on certain aspects of Jesus' career — his death, for ex-

ample — this passage from The Acts stands as a representative statement of what the earliest church considered to be most significant about Jesus Christ.

But in proclaiming the message about Jesus, the preachers were not content with the bare outline; they had to know more about what he said and did to convince their hearers of his significance, and to instruct converts in the Christian way of life. Accordingly, sayings of Jesus and stories about him were treasured by the earliest Christians and handed on from person to person as the faith spread. For about a generation (until nearly A.D. 70), transmission by word of mouth was adequate to fulfill the evangelistic and instructional needs of the newborn church. If a preacher wanted to show how Jesus befriended sinners and outcasts, he would tell a story like that of the visit with Zacchaeus, the tax collector (Luke, ch. 19). To demonstrate how Jesus was able to defeat the powers of evil, an account of his casting out a demon was appropriate. Moral issues arose as well, and here a saying of Jesus' or a story about him could serve as a guide in reaching a decision. In addition to these practical necessities, Christians from earliest times have been interested in the kind of person Jesus was. They have wanted to hear about his compassion, his authority, how he routed his opponents. So, although we do not have a biography of Jesus in the modern sense of the word, revealing stories about him were preserved in the memory of the church and passed on by word of mouth.

Although modern man may be no less interested in these stories about Jesus than the first Christians were, he is often less credulous than his first-century counterpart. The question about the credibility of the Gospel accounts, therefore, has to be faced at the outset.

When a thoughtful reader encounters in the Gospels such stories as those of demonic possession, walking on water, raising the dead, he asks himself: Are the Gospels historically reliable? How central to the Christian faith are such difficult matters as the resurrection, miracles, demons, future judgment, and the end of the world? Must they be believed literally? Perhaps we can approach an understanding of these important problems by raising two basic questions: (1) What do we mean by "historical"? (2) How do we handle the conflict between modern science and the prescientific view of the world which the Gospel writers held?

WHAT REALLY HAPPENED?

Most of us assume that there is no question about what we mean by "historical." If we say something is historical, we mean, "It happened." In a sense that is true, but *not everything that happens is historical*. Untold millions of occurrences "happen" every day that have no relationship to human existence (such as dead trees falling in forests). Others involve human existence but have no significance beyond the occurrences themselves (such as a commuter reading the sports page). Occurrences like these, although they *happen,* can scarcely be regarded as *historical*. To be considered as historical, an event must have some wider meaning for human life.

But as soon as we begin to talk about meanings, we are in an area where the point of view of the observer is of paramount importance. Australian aborigines would undoubtedly regard the Battle of Gettysburg as unworthy of notice, since it has no bearing on their existence. We, in turn, would treat their tribal warfare as insignificant. But even among those directly involved in an event, there is widespread difference in interpretation. Some Americans still speak of the conflict that divided the United States in the 1860's as the "War Between the States," while others refer to it as the "Civil War." The battles were the same for both groups; the difference lies in the standpoint of the observer. Or to put it another way, history is never simply a matter of " what happened "; it always involves what an event meant to a particular person.

But men never arrive at an interpretation of an event in isolation from others. A man is influenced in his interpretation by his family background, his place in society, his education, his philosophical and religious convictions, crude and disorganized though they may be. Construction starts on a new church, and one man says: " Another parasite on the economy." A second man says, " Churchgoing seems to be the thing to do around here; maybe I'd be smart if I joined up." A third swells with pride because he is on the building committee for the new edifice, but a fourth laments: " These rich churches don't preach the old-fashioned religion any more. The church is going to the dogs! " Here are four completely different perspectives on one church building, each determined by the social or ideological group within which each observer has chosen to take his stand.

The group within which the observer takes his stand is of paramount importance in estimating the historical value of the Gospels. Those who preserved the traditions about Jesus were not interested in what we might call an " objective account " of these events; they wanted to convince their hearers of the transforming power and purpose of God which he had revealed through Jesus Christ. If we mean by " historical " something like a newspaper report of happenings long ago, then the Gospels have no interest in historical matters. But if we think of " historical " as meaning events that have significance for human existence, then the Gospels are historical in the highest degree.

Not only are the events connected with Jesus Christ meaningful, in the sense that they are comprehensible and interesting; but they are " meaning-full " in that they enable man to

understand the meaning of his own existence: why God created him; why he sometimes feels like an outsider in the midst
of familiar surroundings; why he is aware of barriers between
himself and other persons and between himself and God;
whether or not evil and death win out in the end. These are
life's ultimate questions; man finds the meaning of his own
life when he finds in the gospel of Jesus Christ the answers to
these questions.

But the meaning to be found in the historical accounts of
Jesus is not a purely individual matter; it shows man that he
can find meaning in his own life only when he takes his stand
within a group, a community of faith, a people. The term
"New Testament," or more properly "New Covenant," refers to the Christian conviction that Jesus came to establish
a new basis on which man may join with his fellows in common devotion to God and common dedication to obey God's
will. Ancient Israel had entered into a covenant at Sinai, as it
is reported in the Old Testament (Ex., ch. 19), but instead of
being a light to the nations, Israel became concerned solely
with herself. Jesus' indictment of his fellow Jews was precisely
at the point of their exclusivism. And he was condemned because he failed to observe the requirements of Jewish exclu-
siveness and insisted on befriending social and religious outcasts. We shall see in subsequent chapters how importantly this
element figures in Jesus' teachings and in his conflicts with the
rabbinic teachers. Here it is enough to observe that Christians
were from the outset a community, sharing common convictions about the meaning of Christ, about the truth God had
revealed through him, about God's purpose for his people and
for the establishment of his Kingdom over all creation.

The Gospel writers all speak from within this community
of faith, and from that perspective they report what Jesus said
and did. Jesus' success in casting out demons is considered by

his enemies as a sign that he is in league with Satan; but his followers are convinced that it shows that God's power is uniquely upon him to enable him to overcome these evil spirits (Luke 11:14-22). There is no suggestion that nothing really happened. The issue is: By what power or authority did it occur? What does it mean, if anything?

DID THE MIRACLES OCCUR?

The Gospels assume — and they are confirmed even by the hostile reports of Jesus in the rabbinic sources — that extraordinary events occurred in connection with the public ministry of Jesus. The rabbis regarded him as a magician; the Christians acclaimed him as the anointed of God. By the time the Gospels were written down, the church had heightened the miraculous element in some of the stories about Jesus, but this tendency to expand supernatural detail can usually be detected by a comparison of the different accounts of the same story. For example, in Mark, Jesus heals a blind man near Jericho (Mark 10:46-52); in Matthew, he heals *two* blind men (Matt. 20:30-34). In Mark, a young man in a white robe is sitting in the empty tomb of Jesus on Easter morning (Mark 16:5); in Matthew, an angel descends from heaven with an appearance like lightning, and raiment white as snow (Matt. 28:3).

The miraculous element in the Gospels is quite modest when compared with the fantastic stories about Jesus found in later books which were never accepted by the church as authoritative. In the so-called Gospel of Thomas, for example, Jesus uses miraculous powers for unworthy ends. When he is challenged for having made some clay pigeons on the Sabbath, he simply claps his hands and orders the pigeons to fly away. In another legend, when some of Jesus' playmates hide from him, he turns them into goats, but later relents and allows them to assume human form again. In contrast to these preposterous legends, our Gospels are quite restrained on the subject of miracles. But even if we acknowledge that the miraculous element in the Gospels has been expanded, there remains a solid core of tradition that credits Jesus with extraordinary powers and actions. The question that confronts us, therefore, is not *whether* the miracles happened, but *by what power* they were performed and what they mean.

Our focus has now shifted from the wider issue of the historicity of the Gospels to the narrower one of the credibility of the miraculous. First, however, we have to decide what we mean by *miracle*. In common usage, it is the suspension of natural law by divine action. But the Biblical writers had no concept of natural law. The universe for them did not function by unchanging laws that God had built into his creation and that would continue in effect of their own accord until he chose to suspend them. Rather, in every moment God is sustaining the universe. Nature is stable and dependable because God is trustworthy and steadfast, not because of inexorable natural laws. When God chooses to act in some extraordinary way, he discloses some special purpose or meaning.

At this point the issues of the historicity of the Gospels and of the miraculous come together. Neither the story of Jesus' life and teachings nor the accounts of his miracles are treated by the writers of the Gospels as proofs of his divinity or as unquestionable demonstrations of his Messiahship. The writers of the Gospels — especially the writer of the Gospel of John (ch. 20:31) — want their readers to be convinced " that Jesus is the Christ, the Son of God," but they report faithfully that many of the original observers of Jesus' mighty works denounced him as controlled by the devil, as a blasphemer, as a subverter of Judaism. But for the man who takes his stand within the community of faith, the meaning of the miracles and of God's message through them becomes as apparent now as it was to Jesus' original circle of followers. Because the lives of men were transformed by the power that they saw at work in Jesus' mighty acts, they were convinced that he was the Christ, the Anointed One of God.

We are now in a position to suggest another dimension of the answer to the question raised at the opening of the chapter as to whether or not the Gospels are historical. They are historical: (1) in the sense that they bear witness to a life lived in the eastern Roman provinces during the early days of the Empire, a life acknowledged by friend and foe as having been accompanied by extraordinary occurrences; (2) in the sense that men found and still find in this person and this life of Jesus Christ the meaning of their own existences; and (3) in the sense that the records of this life, preserved for us in the Gospels, are interpretations, just as any historical document is an interpretation of events it reports and is written from a particular point of view. Such a statement does not guarantee that everything reported in the Gospels happened exactly as a modern reporter who prides himself on his objectivity would have reported it. Some may not have happened at all as they are reported. Obviously there would be sharply divergent interpretations of the events that did occur. The Gospels point, not merely to what happened, but to what it meant to the community of faith, and to the way that it changed the lives of men of faith. It is through their eyes that we must seek to look at the Gospels, in an attempt to see Jesus as they saw him, and to see ourselves in the light of his impact upon them.

Is There a Devil?

We deceive ourselves and undercut the timeless power of the gospel, however, if we insist that in order to understand the truth of Christian faith we must be willing to accept first-century scientific perspectives. What is required is to distinguish between (1) the Biblical writer's picture of the world and (2) his perspective on it. A New Testament writer *pictures the world* in terms of his prescientific world view: hell beneath, a flat earth around him, heaven above him, in the upper reaches of which God dwells. The space among the stars, and even the world around him, was populated by spirits. These could obey God and serve a beneficent function, or they could rebel against him and become the tools of Satan, God's chief adversary. Modern man finds it difficult, if not impossible, to accept this picture as literally true.

But other aspects of the Biblical record have continuing validity in spite of changing scientific views. These include the Biblical writer's *perspective on the world* — that is, his understanding of himself in relation to the Creation, to God, and to the evil powers. The New Testament points to truths that are as fresh and pertinent in the twentieth century as they were in the first: man is dependent for his existence and for the sustaining of his life upon God, his creator; man's life is shaped not only by his individual decisions but by forces that come to him from outside and that may harass or distort his existence; man's destiny is not to be discovered within the limitations of life as he now knows it. God has given him the promise of life that transcends the limits of what he now experiences as life. The creation is not indifferent but good, and God's purpose for it and in it will be brought to fulfillment. God's nature as love and his intention to reconcile all men to himself have been made known in the earthly life of Jesus of Nazareth, whom he has designated as the Christ.

Each of these affirmations is made in the New Testament in language that employs the thought forms of the primitive world picture sketched briefly above. But the theological meaning of the Biblical statements is discernible behind and beyond the prescientific language. One does not have to believe in literal demons to appreciate the sense of release that the demoniacs experienced in their encounters with Jesus and his word of deliverance. The presence and power of these " demonic " influences which limit and threaten man's existence are still a part of man's universal experience, in spite of the antiquated thought forms in which the New Testament describes them.

WILL THE WORLD COME TO AN END?

Another pervasive, yet troublesome, theme in the Gospels is the expectation that the present state of affairs in the world is coming to an end. The New Testament man thinks of time as having a beginning and an end, or at least of the age of the world's history in which he lives as nearing its close. The end is not pictured as the obliteration of the world but as a cataclysmic change that will end one order of the world's existence and institute a new age. The " end " is usually described as accompanied by the return of Christ, the Last Judgment, the resurrection, etc.

A major difficulty with this conception of the end is not merely the rational problem of trying to conceive how such events could occur, but the historical and theological questions created by the fact that these events did not occur when the early church thought they would. The last book of the Bible to be written, II Peter, is still struggling with the problem of the nonfulfillment of the church's expectation of the Second Coming of Christ (II Peter 3:1-13). Paul expected the resurrection to take place during his own lifetime (I Thess. 4:15). Jesus is reported as expecting the end to occur within the lifetime of his own generation (Mark 9:1; 13:30). Albert Schweitzer, in his book *The Quest of the Historical Jesus,* concludes that Jesus expected the consummation of the age to take place within the space of a few weeks, before his disciples could have completed a preaching tour of the villages of Israel. What validity can such an expectation have for us if it failed to be fulfilled at the time when it first arose?

Some theologians have dealt with this problem by treating it as a part of the primitive Jewish understandings of the day — like the three-storied universe — which Jesus used to convey his message to the people of his time. All this business about the coming of the Son of Man sounds bizarre in a prosaic and science-minded day like ours. Other theologians, unwilling to dismiss the idea of the Second Coming and its attendant features as primitive, have sought to transform hopes like these into timeless truths. Passages referring to the Second Coming of Christ really mean, we are told, that he comes to be with his people whenever they gather for worship, or he comes in the Communion, or he comes at death. Similarly, the resurrection is viewed by some contemporary scholars, not as an event of the future, but as an event that takes place repeatedly in the experience of a man of faith when he decides to repudiate the claims of the world upon him. By this decision, he becomes spiritually dead to this life and enters into a new mode of life (i.e., " the resurrection life "). Since a decision like this has such far-reaching consequences for his spiritual life, it is equated with " the judgment " by theologians of this persuasion, who point out that the Greek word translated " judgment " can also mean " decision."

If the hope of the early Christians is being fulfilled repeatedly in the experience of men and women of faith, then there is no problem in the fact that there was not a catastrophic event at a single point in time when the fulfillment occurred. But such a solution is too easy. Furthermore, it does not deal adequately with the New Testament evidence itself. There can be no avoiding the fact that the New Testament writers expected that the present age would come to an end, accompanied by the return of Christ, the resurrection, and the judgment. These events were expected to take place in historical time, not merely in some timeless, spiritual sphere.

This is not, however, merely a problem. The Biblical message about judgment and the age to come furnishes the ground for both warning and assurance. First the *warning:* the message about the impending end of the age reminds us that we cannot establish the Kingdom of God by our efforts or vanquish the powers of evil by our schemes. Here, then, is an effective safeguard against unwarranted optimism or self-confidence. The New Testament teaching about the judgment reminds us that God holds us accountable for our actions. Under his scrutiny we are fully responsible to him for what we do with our lives and how we affect the lives of others.

But there are notes of *assurance* as well. The belief in the resurrection gives us hope that man's existence is not restricted to the limits of life as he now knows it, but that God's eternal purpose in creating man will be fulfilled in spite of the awesomely powerful realities of sickness and death. The expectation of the judgment brings promise that God will one day vindicate the oppressed and bring to account the wicked, the indifferent, the irresponsible.

The time when these expectations will be fulfilled and the circumstances under which they will take place are unknown and of secondary importance. Jesus refused to commit himself on the timing of the day of consummation of this age (Mark 13:32), even though he was so convinced that it *would* come that he predicted that some of his followers would live to see it. *That* there will be a day of fulfillment is the universal New Testament affirmation; the conditions of the fulfillment are not presented with any consensus, much less with a fixed timing. The focus falls throughout the New Testament on the decisive difference that Jesus Christ has already made: his life, death, and resurrection give assurance that God will bring to completion his purposes.

DID JESUS RISE FROM THE DEAD?

Of the various aspects of the time of fulfillment, the most frequently mentioned, and the most difficult to comprehend, is the resurrection. The whole idea of a resurrection is so completely beyond the range of our experience that we feel we must either reject the idea or discard rationality in accepting it. Part of the problem lies in the misconception of what the New Testament actually teaches about the resurrection. It nowhere suggests that a resurrection is simply bringing a corpse back to life. Paul, who has more to say on the subject than any other New Testament writer, specifically excludes this understanding of the resurrection. He writes: " It is sown a physical body, it is raised a spiritual body." (I Cor. 15:44.)

The Greek word translated " body " does not mean the material substance of the individual as distinguished from his mind, spirit, or soul. Although at times the word does mean the part of man that can be touched, its primary meaning is closely related to our English word " self." The Gospel writers would agree that the " self " survives into the resurrection, not as a physical " self " but as a spiritual " self." We wish we knew exactly what Paul meant by a " spiritual self," but we must confess that we do not. It is clear that he did not mean simply a revived corpse, nor did he refer to a disembodied spirit. It seems to be his way of saying that in the resurrection the *real self* is preserved and transformed by God's act, to become what God intended man to be when He created him.

The stories of the resurrection of Jesus in the Gospels insist that the resurrected Christ is recognizably identifiable with Jesus of Nazareth. Yet each of the Gospel accounts suggests that there are also differences between Jesus as an earthly human being and Jesus as raised from the dead. In his resurrection appearances he is depicted as being free from the limitations of merely human life. Any view of the resurrection of Jesus must, therefore, preserve both the sense of continuity between earthly and resurrection life and the element of transformation of earthly life that the resurrection effects. The paramount fact for the New Testament is that God raised Jesus from the dead, as attested by his appearances to members of the community of faith. Questions about the circumstances or details of the resurrection are simply not discussed.

Yet the encounter by his followers with Jesus Christ, risen from the dead, is the capstone of the gospel. If Jesus' followers had not met him in the resurrection, there would have been no community of faith, no significance attached to his death (except that of a bitter tragedy), or to his teachings (except that of an erratic and indiscreet amateur rabbi). Because they did meet him, they understood the meaning of his life and death. And above all, they were filled with a zeal to tell to others the good news of what God had revealed through Jesus Christ and of the purpose that he was about to fulfill. The assurance that he would fulfill that purpose was given when God raised Jesus from the dead, and in the light of that assurance they went out to preach the gospel. In their mission to preach the gospel and to instruct the faithful who responded to it, they produced the powerful little books that we know as the Gospels.

CHAPTER 2 | *From the Gospel to the Gospels*

In the last chapter we saw that the kerygma provided the basic framework for the Gospels, and that the selection of material to be included in the Gospels was influenced by the teaching and preaching needs of the early church. But why could not one Gospel have served adequately to communicate the gospel? Why were there as many as four? How are we to account for the differences among them? When they disagree with each other in detail, as we must honestly acknowledge that they do, how are we to decide which one is more nearly accurate? If one of Jesus' followers had written down what he said and did while it was happening or shortly thereafter, we should now have one authoritative account. But instead, we have four distinctively different Gospels.

DIFFERENCES AMONG THE GOSPELS

No two of the Gospels begin in precisely the same way, and no two end alike. Superficially, it could be said that both Matthew and Luke begin with stories of Jesus' birth. From years of watching Christmas pageants and hearing Christmas cantatas, we have fused these two accounts in our minds, but they are quite different in detail. The angels, the shepherds, the manger, the census, the return to the native town of Naza-

reth, are found only in Luke (ch. 2:1-39). In Matthew, Bethlehem is the home of Mary and Joseph, and they have their own
house where Jesus was born and where the Magi visited. The
flight into Egypt and the move to Nazareth were to escape the
wrath of the Herodian kings (Matt. 1:18 to 2:23). Although
the first incidents recorded in both Mark and John concern
contacts between Jesus and John the Baptist, there is little real
similarity between the accounts. In Mark, Jesus is baptized by
John and commissioned by God (Mark 1:1-11); in John, Jesus
is acclaimed by John, but is not baptized (John 1:19-34). Even
more strikingly different is the majestic prologue with which
John's Gospel opens, announcing the theme of the eternal
Word of God that has become incarnate in Jesus of Nazareth.
John and Mark make no mention of the birth of Jesus.

The differences among the Gospels extend to details. In
some cases, one Gospel will provide important supplements
to the others. For example, only in Luke do we have some of
Jesus' best-known parables: the prodigal son, the good Samaritan, the rich man and Lazarus, the Pharisee and the publican.
Only Matthew preserves the parable of the Last Judgment and
the parable of the ten maidens (Matt., ch. 25). But the Gospels
differ among themselves not only in supplementing each other
or in offering special accounts of certain incidents (like the
birth of Jesus), but in minute detail.

Often the detail is of no great consequence in itself, but the
very fact that it is there raises a question as to how it originated. In the story of the raising of Jairus' daughter, for example, Mark tells us that the child was at the point of death
when her father came to Jesus (Mark 5:23). The drama of the
story depends in part on the delay of Jesus in reaching Jairus'
home, for by that time the child has died, and Jesus must restore her to life. But in Matthew's version of the story (Matt.
9:18), the child is already dead when Jairus comes to Jesus so

that the delay loses its point. There is, of course, no great significance in this disagreement between Mark and Matthew, but it raises for us the question as to how such differences could have arisen.

Differences among the Gospels can also be found in their reports of Jesus' sayings. Even in such a familiar passage as the Lord's Prayer, Matthew (ch. 6:9-13) and Luke (ch. 11:2-4) have quite different versions (and see the two forms of the Beatitudes in Matt. 5:3-12; Luke 6:20-23). Any careful study of the Gospels must be ready to explain the variety of forms in which the traditions about Jesus have been handed down.

The basic fact to be recognized is that there were no written Gospels until about forty years after Jesus' public ministry. In that extended period, the stories about Jesus and the recollections of what he had said were preserved in the memory of the church and transmitted by word of mouth. The differences among the Gospels arose, therefore, both in the process of oral transmission and in the process of reproducing the traditions in written form.

THE GOSPEL BY WORD OF MOUTH

The process of transmitting the gospel materials by word of mouth tended to give them a fixed pattern, since such a definite form would be an aid to memory. For example, a story of healing often began with an account of the state of the afflicted, followed by details about the length of the period of suffering or the inability of physicians to deal with it in the ordinary way. Then came the encounter with Jesus, in which he spoke a word or called for some response. The story ended with an account of the cure and an expression of amazement from the observers. A good example of this form appears in Mark 5:1-20, where we read about Jesus casting a troop of demons out of a man. First, there are details about the hopelessness and degradation of his condition (vs. 1-5), living in tombs and unable to be bound even with chains. Then follows a description of his initial hostility to Jesus (vs. 6-7). The word of Jesus commanding the demons to come out of him and sending them into the herd of swine is the climax of the incident (vs. 8-13). The account concludes with the amazement of the people (including the herdsmen who had lost their swine!), and the calm, joyful state of the man who had been cured (vs. 14-20).

The sayings of Jesus, especially his parables, similarly tended to fall into stylized forms in the process of oral transmission. Once the modern reader identifies these patterns, he can sometimes distinguish between what may have been the original form of a saying or story and the form in which it now appears in one of the Gospels. When such a distinction is possible, it is doubly illuminating: it not only shows us what was probably the original form of a saying of Jesus' or a story about him, but it also tells us something about the Christian community that preserved this tradition. In Mark 10:11, for example, Jesus unequivocally rejects divorce and remarriage. But in Matt. 5:32, which is clearly the same saying, an exception is allowed: divorce is permitted if one party is guilty of adultery. From this difference between Mark and Matthew, we learn how stringent Jesus' saying on this subject was, and how, by the time Matthew's material was taking shape, the church was no longer able to hold to the rigid moral standard set by Jesus himself. It is rarely possible to determine whether such modifications of the sayings of Jesus are the work of the Gospel writer himself or are the result of the point of view that prevailed in the community in which the saying was remembered. But in some cases, the characteristic additions of the Gospel writer are easily identified. For example, in his versions of the parables, Matthew seemingly takes delight in adding a comment about the wicked " weeping and gnashing their

teeth " or being " cast . . . into outer darkness " (Matt. 13:42,
50; 25:30). In each such instance, Matthew diverges from Mark
and Luke.

It is difficult for twentieth-century man to realize that the
practice of preserving the stories and sayings of Jesus in oral
form only was not a matter of carelessness but was intentional.
The whole tradition among the rabbinic interpreters of the
Jewish law was to carry on the teachings of the great rabbis
solely by memorization. Every rabbinic student was expected
to remember word for word, not only what his own teacher
taught, but what his teacher's teacher had taught *him*. In
theory, at least, this chain of oral teachings reached back to
Moses himself. The teachings of the rabbis did not begin to be
written down until after the destruction of the Temple in
Jerusalem in A.D. 70, when it appeared that the very founda-
tions of Judaism were in danger.

Although there are some similarities between the method
of preserving rabbinic sayings and the process of preserving
the traditions about Jesus, the differences are considerable. In
the first place, the period of time during which the materials
circulated orally is much shorter in the case of the Christian
traditions, since the last of the four Gospels was probably
written before the end of the first century. Secondly, there is
little if any evidence of Jesus' employing a formal mode of
instruction such as the rabbis used. Many of the sayings and
stories were remembered in different forms by different seg-
ments of the early church, and yet the Christians seem to have
felt no initial embarrassment at producing four Gospels that
differed from each other in sequence of events, in what they
included, and in details. Later, the fathers of the church felt
obligated to explain these differences, and scribes copying the
manuscripts actually tried to harmonize the divergences.

An important instance of such harmonization occurs at Luke

20:19. Luke apparently omitted from his account of the Last Supper mention of the cup Jesus drank after supper, which the other Gospels explain in the familiar words of the Communion service: "This cup which is poured out for you is the new covenant in my blood." Certain copyists, however, thought that these words were too important to be left out, and so they added them. (They appear in the King James Version as Luke 22:20, but the Revised Standard Version places them in a footnote.) At the time the Gospels were written, these divergences seem to have created no difficulty in the eyes of the church.

A third area of difference between the rabbis and the early Christians in the matter of oral tradition involves the motivation each group had for preserving the tradition in this way. The rabbis took delight in the fluid, dynamic atmosphere that the oral method created, since it allowed for constant readaptation of the otherwise fixed law of Moses. Not a letter, not a stroke of a letter, of the written code could be changed. But the rabbinic interpreters could, through orally transmitted interpretations, alter the force of the fixed statutes in an almost unlimited number of ways. On the other hand, the early Christians were so certain that the end of the age was coming momentarily that they did not trouble to write down for posterity what Jesus had said and done. One suspects also that some of the earliest leaders of the church did not know how to read and write, since in Acts 4:13, the word translated as "uneducated" means "illiterate." The fathers of the church who recorded the traditions about the origins of the New Testament writings report that Peter relied on Mark to write down his recollections of the teachings and activities of Jesus. Obviously a man like Paul would have had the learning to prepare written records of the gospel traditions, but since there seemed to be no need for written accounts, none were made until the first generation of Christians began to pass away.

First Steps Toward Written Records

The event that seems to have convinced the church that the time had come to preserve its traditions in written form was the Roman siege of Jerusalem culminating in the destruction of the Temple (A.D. 68–70). Although it is impossible to recover the details of what happened to the church at this time, it appears that the official attitude of Judaism toward the Christians in Jerusalem began to change about A.D. 62, when the high priest executed James, the brother of Jesus and the head of the Jerusalem church. The high priest's hostility may have been directed solely toward James, whose popularity he resented, but the consequence of his action was a mounting antagonism between Jew and Christian. Christians began to interpret the impending destruction of Jerusalem by the Romans as the hand of God, visiting judgment on the Jews for their rejection of Jesus as Messiah. The situation in Jerusalem became intolerable for the Christians, who, according to the ancient church historian Eusebius, fled for safety to the Gentile city of Pella, on the eastern side of the Jordan River. Many scholars think that the crisis depicted in Mark, ch. 13, is reported in the light of the impending destruction of Jerusalem and its Temple.

Another possible explanation for the decision to write down the traditions about Jesus is also plagued by historical uncertainties. If it is true that Peter's recollections about Jesus were recorded by Mark, the crisis that may have impelled the Christians to record the stories and sayings of Jesus may have been the persecution of the Roman Christians by the emperor Nero in A.D. 64. We cannot now be sure whether the specific event that led to the formulation of the first connected account of Jesus' ministry and message was the death of James in Jerusalem or the death of Peter in Rome or something else completely unknown to us. But for reasons which we shall examine in a moment we can be certain that Mark was the first of the Gospels to be written.

At the same time, a case can be made for the theory that there were other documents in use before the first of the Gospels was written, and that these came to be incorporated in whole or in part in the Gospels as we now have them. Since so much of each of the Gospels is devoted to a fairly detailed account of the closing days of Jesus' life, and especially to the circumstances of his death, it is possible that there were in use among preachers documents detailing his sufferings and death, called Passion narratives (from Latin *passus,* " suffering ").

Another suggestion is that the early church made collections of the sayings of Jesus, and that the existence of such collections can be traced by simple literary detective work in our present Gospels. The ideal tool for this kind of investigation is a book that prints the first three Gospels — for convenience they are called the Synoptic Gospels — in parallel columns so that the reader can see at a glance the relationships in content and order among the three. (Since the Gospel of John is completely different in both order and content from the other three, except in some of the Passion narrative, it has to be considered separately.) The Revised Standard Version of the Synoptic Gospels is published in this comparative form under the title *Gospel Parallels* (Thomas Nelson & Sons, 1949). When the Gospels are read in this manner, it becomes evident that the order of events in Mark is adopted with only minor modifications by Matthew and Luke, and that nearly all the contents of Mark are reproduced in Matthew and Luke (the latter has some significant omissions).

But very striking is the fact that Matthew and Luke have a great deal of material in common, mostly sayings, that is not found at all in Mark. This has led scholars to conjecture that

there was an early document, consisting mostly of sayings of
Jesus, which Matthew and Luke drew upon independently
to supplement the material in Mark. Some scholars think that
Mark, too, drew on this source for the Sayings material that
appears in his Gospel. Still others think that there was simply
a fund of remembered sayings of Jesus from which all the
writers of the Gospels drew, a theory that cannot readily explain exact agreement between Matthew and Luke or the fact
that a string of sayings will appear in exactly the same order in
the two Gospels.

The conclusion is that there was probably a document that
included the sayings of Jesus, that it was used independently
by the writers of the First and Third Gospels, and that it fell
into disuse and disappeared after its contents were incorporated
into the Gospels as we now have them. The date of this hypo-
thetical collection has been set as early as A.D. 40, but since we
cannot be certain that it ever existed (nor do we possess even
a manuscript fragment of such a document), no one can dog-
matize about its contents or the date of its origin. To postulate
its existence, however, is useful in explaining the probable
mutual relationships of our Gospels.

WHICH IS THE OLDEST GOSPEL?

As we have noted, the Gospel that seems to have provided
the basic structure for both Matthew and Luke is Mark. Where
Matthew and Luke reproduce Mark, it is often in an abridged
form. Where Mark's phraseology is awkward, Matthew, and
even more Luke, may improve the literary style. Where Mark
reports that the Spirit " drove out " Jesus into the desert (literally, " ejected him," Mark 1:12), Luke says he " was led by
the Spirit " (Luke 4:1). Luke and Matthew have extensive
supplemental material at both the beginning and the end of
Mark's account. Mark begins with the baptism; Matthew and

Luke start with their infancy stories. Mark (in the best Greek manuscripts) ends with the women fearful at the empty tomb; Matthew and Luke have extended accounts of the appearances of the risen Christ. It is clear that Luke and Matthew have (1) reproduced Mark's narratives, often in an abridged form, and (2) supplemented his material with sayings and a few narratives, partly from a common source, and partly from their own special sources.

If we accept the theory that Mark is the oldest Gospel, and that Matthew and Luke independently combined it with material from the Sayings Source (called Q, for *Quelle,* the German word meaning " source "), we still have not accounted for the distinctive features of Matthew and Luke, with respect to both their order and content. Matthew is a somewhat easier case, since he includes nearly the whole of Mark and follows Mark's order rather closely. He has supplemented it, of course, with materials that are uniquely his own, such as the Last Judgment (Matt. 25:31-46), the stories of the Magi (Matt. 2:1-12) and of the slaughter of the innocents (ch. 2:13-18), the parable of the ten virgins (ch. 25:1-13), and some parables of the Kingdom (ch. 13:24-30, 36-50). But with Luke, the questions are far more complicated.

Although, in the over-all structure of his Gospel, Luke follows Mark's order, at several points where Matthew follows Mark, Luke omits extended narrative sections of Mark. Examples of this appear in the account of the death of John the Baptist (Mark 6:17-29; Matt. 14:3-12), and in the entire passage from Mark 6:45 to 8:10 (Matt. 14:22 to 15:39). Luke shows similar independence in the passages where he and Matthew are parallel (i.e., in the Q sections). Luke's Passion narrative differs in many details from Mark's, which is followed quite closely in Matthew. And in Luke 9:51 to 18:14 is a great deal of material to be found only in this Gospel.

In Luke some of the sayings of Jesus seem to be reproduced in a more primitive form than Matthew reports them. For example, the Beatitudes in Matt., ch. 5, have a liturgical quality about them as though they had assumed that form as a part of the worship practice of a Christian community. This is contrasted with the simpler form of Luke: Matthew has " Blessed are the poor in spirit," where Luke has " Blessed are you poor." Some scholars have suggested that Luke's Gospel first consisted of a combination of Luke's own source with the Sayings Source. At a later time Luke came across Mark and expanded his Gospel with material drawn from Mark. Whether this theory is correct or not, the fact remains that Luke is freer in his use of Mark than Matthew is, and he often reports the sayings of Jesus in a more primitive form than the one Matthew preserves.

Throughout this discussion we have been using the names " Matthew," " Mark," and " Luke " to describe the " writers " of the Gospels, and necessity requires that we do so. But it should be recognized that none of the Gospels indicates who its author was, and we have only traditions of questionable authority to go on. There is a possibility that the Gospels were not written by individuals at all, or at least that the persons who gave them their present form were more editors than authors. But whether prepared by individuals or not, each one developed in a particular Christian community and embodied the traditions about Jesus preserved in the corporate memory and experience of that community. The fact that each of the Gospels has certain words and phrases that it favors would indicate that each Gospel had a final editor who put it in its present form. And in the case of " Luke," there is clear evidence of a self-conscious literary effort on the part of the anonymous writer, who addresses his two-volume work (the book of The Acts is part two) to his patron, Theophilus (Luke 1:3; Acts 1:1).

For details of the special aims and structure of the Gospels we must examine each of them individually. But the differences among the four Gospels must not obscure the fact that they were written with a common objective in mind: to convey to the reader the good news that in Jesus Christ God was fulfilling his purpose through his new people.

| *The Gospel of the Son of God: Mark*

T<small>HE</small> Gospel According to Mark is the oldest of our four Gospels and is associated in ancient tradition with Peter and with Rome. According to an early second-century account, Mark was Peter's companion in Rome, and recorded Peter's recollections of what Jesus had said and done.

This tradition receives some support from the fact that Peter is the most important of the disciples in Mark's account. He is the first disciple to be called; his mother-in-law is among those healed at Capernaum; he is the spokesman for the disciples on most occasions, including the confession of Jesus' Messiahship (Mark 8:29); and it is Peter who is singled out by name when the young man tells the disciples to go to Galilee to meet the risen Christ (ch. 16:7). The central place given to Peter may indicate only that he was the acknowledged leader of the twelve disciples, but it may also demonstrate that the writer of Mark had a special interest in Peter.

One feature of Mark suggests a close connection with Palestinian Christianity. He frequently quotes words or phrases in Aramaic, the language spoken by Jesus. Examples of this are *Talitha cumi* (ch. 5:41), *Corban* (ch. 7:11), *Ephphatha* (ch. 7:33), none of which occur in Matthew or Luke. Although the use of Aramaic words and expressions does not prove that these stories are historically trustworthy, it heightens the probability that they go back to Jesus' original circle of Aramaic-speaking followers.

The primary objective of Mark's Gospel is, of course, to proclaim the gospel. As we observed in the first chapter, the outline of the kerygma and the outline of Mark are parallel. And although Mark's account of Jesus is by no means complete, and it makes no claim to record the exact chronological order, the essential elements of the kerygma are there in Mark in their proper order: Jesus' ministry begins with his baptism by John; it gets under way in Galilee, where he preaches and casts out demons; it comes to a turning point when the crowds begin to resent him but his disciples recognize him as Messiah; its dramatic climax comes when Jesus is tried and executed, only to be raised by God's power from the dead. The gospel, for Mark, is not only something Jesus preached, and certainly not merely something the disciples later said about Jesus. It includes what he was, how he lived, what he did, how people responded to him, the death he died, and the new life God made available through him.

JESUS AND THE CLAIM TO BE MESSIAH

In proclaiming the gospel, therefore, Mark is eager to stress that Jesus is the Messiah. But the meaning of the word " Messiah " is not so simple as it may seem. It is a Hebrew term that means " Anointed [One]." (" Christ " comes from the Greek equivalent.) But anointed for what and by whom? And what does anointing signify? We cannot assume that the New Testament means by " Messiah " exactly what the term meant to Jesus' Jewish contemporaries. The reverse is true; Jesus did not fit any of the Jewish definitions of Messiah. Or more accurately, the Christian understanding of Jesus as Messiah combines several forms of the Jewish expectation.

The Son of Man. In Mark's Gospel, Jesus never applies to himself the term "Messiah." He allows Peter's identifying him as Messiah to stand (ch. 8:29), and he answers the high priest affirmatively when asked directly if he is the Christ (ch. 14:61). But Jesus apparently preferred to refer to himself as the Son of Man. This could be a way of avoiding the use of the pronoun "I," since the Aramaic term "Son of Man" could mean simply "a man," or "I." But the phrase "Son of Man" was also used in Dan. 7:13-18 and in the Book of Enoch to designate a chosen, heavenly agent of God who would deliver his people and overcome the evil powers.

Now it makes a great deal of difference whether Jesus was using this phrase as a sign of his humility or as a claim to a unique role in the fulfillment of God's purpose. In recent years, some scholars have tried to get around this difficulty by saying that passages that use "Son of Man" as equivalent to "I" are authentic (such as Mark 2:10, where this interpretation makes sense). On the other hand, these scholars claim that the sayings that report Jesus as thinking of himself as the Son of Man in a redemptive sense (such as ch. 9:12) originated later in the church. Passages in which Jesus speaks of the Son of Man as yet to come (ch. 13:36, for example) are considered authentic, but they suggest that Jesus was talking about someone else who was to come, not about himself. There are two major difficulties with this attempt to dismiss Jesus' claims to be the Son of Man. (1) In the very passages where he speaks of the Son of Man as a coming figure (for example, ch. 8:38), man's destiny in the day of the Son of Man's coming is determined by his response to Jesus in this age. Jesus, if he is not the Son of Man, is the more important personage of the two! The simpler interpretation of the passages is that Jesus, as coming Son of Man, executes judgment on men in accordance with their response to him now. (2) The passages in which "Son of Man " can be translated as " I " do not reduce the phrase to a self-effacing way by which a man identifies himself. Rather, they present Jesus as making astounding claims for himself, forgiving sins (ch. 2:10) or exercising Lordship over the Sabbath (v. 28), for example. The most plausible explanation for these statements is that Jesus sensed that God had designated him for the mission of bringing in the new age in which God's people would be reconstituted and his will would prevail over all men. Conscious of this commissioning, he identified his role in terms of the traditional Jewish title: the Son of Man.

The Suffering Servant. Even so, the Son of Man in the Gospels does not fit neatly into the Jewish expectation. The Jews expected him to triumph; Mark reports that Jesus knew he must suffer (chs. 8:31; 9:12). At this point the new element in Jesus' understanding of his mission appears: the triumph over evil and the establishment of the new people of God can be achieved only through suffering and death. Mark 9:12 is the key passage on this subject: " How is it written of the Son of man, that he should suffer many things and be treated with contempt? " The fact is that no such statement about the Son of Man appears in the Old Testament. The allusion to suffering seems to come from Isa., ch. 53, which describes the Servant of the Lord, not the Son of Man. Jesus has combined these two themes in his own creative synthesis, in response to his " anointing " by God.

The Messianic Secret. Interpreters of Mark often speak of the " Messianic secret," implying that Jesus' repeated command to his followers and to the demons not to reveal his identity explains why not even his inner circle of followers believed firmly in his Messiahship until the resurrection. If he had claimed to be Messiah, his disciples would have had no doubts about it. After the resurrection experiences, the Messianic claim was read back into the record of his ministry but was treated as though he had kept it a secret.

The difficulties with this widely influential theory are very great. Jesus was clearly condemned as a Messianic pretender, although his understanding of Messiahship was completely different from the political meaning it had for the authorities. There is no accounting for the emergence of faith in him as a crucified Messiah (a contradiction in terms to the Jewish outlook of the day) unless he made some Messianic claims during his lifetime. The crux of the matter lies in Jesus' radical reinterpretation of Messiahship. He refused to allow people to call him Messiah, if they meant a leader of nationalistic revolt. His own sense of mission involved the role of the Servant who suffered and the Son of Man who established the new people of God and triumphed over God's enemies. For this he believed God had anointed him.

THE PATTERN OF MARK'S GOSPEL

In addition to the general pattern of Mark's Gospel derived from the kerygma, there are certain clearly marked divisions in the book. In some cases the divisions are marked by geographical shifts in the story; in other cases they are introduced by significant summary statements. An outline might look like this:

I. Introduction, ch. 1:1-13
   The ministry of John the Baptist; the baptism of Jesus and the temptation.

II. Beginning of the Ministry in Galilee, chs. 1:14 to 3:6
   The theme of Jesus' preaching; the call of the disciples; a typical day in Jesus' ministry of healing; the rise of opposition from within official Judaism.

III. The Climax of the Ministry in Galilee, chs. 3:7 to 6:13
   Summary of the response to Jesus' ministry. Mounting

opposition; the parables of the Kingdom; the miracles; the rejection of Jesus at Nazareth.

IV. The Ministry Extended Beyond Galilee, chs. 6:14 to 8:26
The beginning of governmental opposition; the feeding of the five thousand and a resurgence of popular response; the issue of defilement; withdrawal into Gentile territory and the feeding of the four thousand; the Jewish leaders demand a sign; the obtuseness of the disciples; a blind man receives his sight.

V. The Messiahship Confessed and the Journey to Jerusalem, chs. 8:27 to 10:52
Messiahship involves suffering; the Passion predicted; journey through Gentile regions; the self-seeking disciples; a blind man healed in Jericho.

VI. The Ministry in Jerusalem, chs. 11:1 to 13:37
The cleansing of the Temple; the conflict with Pharisees and Sadducees; "Whose Son is Messiah?"; the predictions of the end of the age.

VII. The Passion and the Resurrection, chs. 14:1 to 16:8
The plot; the Last Supper; the scene in the Garden; the arrest and trial; the crucifixion; the empty tomb and the command to return to Galilee.

(The preceding outline is based on Vincent Taylor's commentary on Mark.)

The materials under these headings are arranged in an order that is more often topical than strictly chronological. Some of the material placed by Mark at the early part of the Gospel, dealing with the conflict between Jesus and the scribes over observance of the law, should almost certainly come at the close of Jesus' career. But many of Mark's frequent references to geographical locations seem to be part of the primitive tradition as it came to him and to preserve accurately hints of locale and movement in Jesus' public ministry.

PREPARE THE WAY OF THE LORD

Mark opens his Gospel with a quotation from the books of
Malachi and Isaiah, reminding us of the strong conviction
among the early Christians that God was fulfilling through
Jesus Christ what he had promised to his people Israel in Old
Testament times.

John appears, baptizing the repentant, in the barren territory
at the northern end of the Dead Sea. A few miles to the south-
west lived the Essene community which produced the Dead
Sea scrolls. They too were baptizers, although there is no evidence that either John or Jesus was ever a part of that community. The stress that John and the Essenes laid on baptism
resulted from dissatisfaction with the spiritual state of Judaism
at the time. John, like the Essenes, rejected the assumption
that a person could consider himself a member of the people
of God merely because he was born a Jew. He must demonstrate his worthiness to be numbered among God's people by
purity of life and a repentant heart.

We cannot be sure what John intended his baptism to signify. Some scholars have suggested that it was the so-called
proselyte baptism, which allowed Gentiles to be baptized and
circumcised in order to qualify for admission to the people
Israel. John would, then, be implying that even Jews were so
far from God that they had to come in the same way as
Gentiles if they were to find their place in God's chosen people. A more plausible suggestion, with some support from the
Dead Sea scrolls, is that John believed, with his contemporaries, that in the Day of Judgment God would send a river
of fire upon the earth to purge from it all evil. If man sub-
mitted to the purifying effects of baptism with water now, he
would be unharmed by the fiery judgment that God would
pour out upon the earth.

Mark gives no indication (ch. 1:4-11) that John saw any difference between Jesus and the large numbers of other devout Jews who came to be baptized in the Jordan. The voice that came from God was, according to Mark, a private disclosure addressed to Jesus only. He was acclaimed as " my beloved Son," which means of course, the Son of God. The idea of a divine being's begetting a son is completely foreign to Hebrew ways of thinking. The closest the Old Testament comes to such a concept is in Psalm 2: " You are my son, today I have begotten you." The reference is probably to a festival in ancient Israel at which the king was enthroned annually on New Year's Day and acclaimed as God's viceroy: that is, as the one who ruled over God's people by his power, in his stead, and, hopefully, in accord with his will. The term " Son of God " was for Jewish Christians a royal term referring to the King as one who exercised authority granted him by God.

But the quotation in Mark is not taken directly from Ps. 2; it also contains hints of the Servant Songs of Second Isaiah (chs. 40 to 55). Actually, there is no direct Messianic reference in the quotation. Some commentators have concluded from this that Jesus was aware of a unique relationship to God before he was aware of the nature of his Messianic mission. The Greek word " son " is a possible translation of the Hebrew word " servant," so that perhaps by seeing himself as the lowly Servant of the Lord, Jesus came to see that his Messiahship involved suffering and eventually death.

When faith in Jesus as Son of God spread out into Greek territory, Gentile Christians immediately associated him with the mystic savior-gods of the Greek religions, who, because they were part human and part divine, could impart divine life to their worshipers. But at the outset, no such language or expectations are associated with the description of Jesus as God's " beloved Son." In Mark's account, the phrase carries the meaning — an exceedingly important one — of one who has a unique role to fulfill in the purpose of God. As we have observed, Jesus' use of the phrase "Son of Man" shows that he was the one through whom God's rule over his creation would be established.

Although Mark has only a brief report of the temptation of Jesus (Mark 1:12-13), we learn from the fuller accounts in Matthew and Luke that the issue in the temptations was the attempt to make Jesus use his extraordinary powers to gain political power and a popular following. The writers of the Gospels locate this temptation at the beginning of Jesus' ministry, as though it were a specific event which occurred only at that particular moment. But we can be sure that this issue plagued him to the end of his career. From all such political proposals, Jesus steadfastly withdrew (see John 6:15).

THE COMING OF THE KINGDOM OF GOD

Jesus' central concern was for the Kingdom of God and its coming. His gospel was "the gospel *of God*" (Mark 1:14-15) because it was the good news that God was beginning to establish his reign over the earth. Every phrase of Mark's summary of Jesus' message is profoundly important.

"*The time is fulfilled.*" Hebrew faith in the God who acts in history carries with it the conviction that God chooses certain crucial points in time at which he reveals himself in a special way. Conveniently, there is a special Greek word for this way of viewing time: *kairos*. This is not merely time as measurable in minutes, hours, days, or years, but time as an eventful moment, the right time, the strategic moment. Israel had looked forward to a day of restitution when God would judge the wicked and vindicate the righteous as a prelude to a new age. Passages in The Book of Isaiah are especially eloquent in depicting this day (Isa., chs. 11; 26; 35; 43). Now, says Jesus, God's hour is about to strike; his rule will be established, his purpose will be fulfilled.

"*The kingdom of God.*" It is common in American Protestant circles to speak of the Kingdom of God as an inner state of mind or a feeling in man's heart. This understanding rests largely on a dubious translation of a single verse (Luke 17:21, RSV, margin): "The kingdom of God is within you." Actually, the verse is discussing the question of "signs," advance indications that the Kingdom is going to arrive. But Jesus declares that there is no advance notice; as quickly as the lightning flashes from one part of the sky to another, so quickly — and unexpectedly — the Kingdom is *in your midst.*

The Kingdom, therefore, is sent by God. It is his manifesting himself in human affairs to bring men into obedience to himself and to overcome the evil powers that seek to thwart his purposes. That is why the conflict of Jesus with the demons is such an important part of the Gospel account. As he is God's agent in overcoming the demonic powers, the Kingdom has already manifested itself in the here and now. "But if it is by the finger of God that I cast out demons, then has the *kingdom of God* come upon you." (Luke 11:20.)

But the Kingdom is not sent merely to individuals. Another important word of Jesus concerning the Kingdom is reported by Luke (ch. 12:32): "Fear not, little flock, for it is your Father's good pleasure to give you the kingdom." The Kingdom is given to the flock, that is, to the people of God. Only from within the perspective of faith of the Christian community are we able to recognize in Jesus' works the powers of God's Kingdom. To the flock has been committed the twofold task of announcing the Kingdom's coming and engaging in the work of reconciliation that is needed to prepare men for its coming.

"... *Is at hand.*" A more literal translation of this phrase would be "has drawn near." But the Greek could mean "the kingdom of God has approached," or it could mean, "the kingdom has arrived." In the light of what the rest of the Gospel has to say about the coming of the Kingdom, it seems to mean: (1) God's time (*kairos*) has arrived, and he is about to act in a decisive way to establish his Kingdom; (2) the powers of the Kingdom and the new possibilities for man's life in the new age are already operative through Jesus and the community that he has called into being; (3) the time when God will bring to consummation his purposes is soon to come, but has not yet fully arrived. God's people, therefore, are living between two times: (1) the time when God has begun to unleash the powers that will overcome evil, and (2) the time when all creation will acknowledge his sovereignty.

"*Repent, and believe in the gospel.*" The word translated as "repent" does not mean "be sorry for past deeds," but "turn, change direction." The prophets called Israel to repent, that is, to return to obedient trust in her God. Here the call is to turn to God, whose purpose and power are now being revealed, and to trust in the mighty acts that he is performing, to which the good news of the gospel bears witness.

AUTHORITY AND OPPOSITION

The distinguishing quality of Jesus' ministry is his authority. He exercises authority over the demons; he interprets the Jewish law in an authoritative manner that is not commonly found among the scribes, the professional interpreters of Judaism in that day. In both cases the reader is made aware that this authority is a manifestation of the Spirit that came from God and descended upon Jesus at the time of his commissioning.

A Typical Day. The first half of the description of a typical day is concerned with the conflict with the demons and the ministry of healing. The demoniacally possessed man (Mark 1:23), apparently conscious of Jesus' mission to overcome the demonic and liberate men from its control, recognizes who Jesus is and what power is at work through him. At Jesus' word, the demon is overcome, to the astonishment of the crowd, who spread Jesus' reputation throughout Galilee. The response is so tremendous that Jesus has difficulty making his way through the villages, and goes out to open country where the crowds can be accommodated.

Although the beneficiaries of Jesus' healing activity include Simon Peter's mother-in-law (ch. 1:29-31), the fullest account of a healing takes place in a house in Capernaum (ch. 2:1-12). The most significant thing about the incident is Jesus' claim to the authority to forgive sins. Opposition to Jesus arises among the scribes when Jesus tells the man his sins are forgiven. What he means, of course, is, " God has forgiven your sins." But in the words that follow, Jesus says that authority on earth to forgive sins has been given to him as Son of Man. Clearly, Jesus associates the man's paralysis with his state of sinfulness; or to put it in modern terms, guilt lies behind his physical disability. Both aspects of the man's problem are dealt with at once: he is forgiven, and he is healed.

The incident introduces a series of stories of controversy which serve to point up the distinctive qualities of Jesus' ministry: he chooses a despised tax collector to be one of his intimate followers (Mark 2:13-14); he eats a meal with persons who are religiously unacceptable and ceremonially impure (vs. 15-17); he encourages joyous social gatherings instead of the solemn, even ascetic, way of life enjoined by strict Judaism and so greatly admired in John the Baptist (vs. 18-22); he supports and joins his disciples when they violate the ancient law of Sabbath observance, on the ground that human need is more important than religious observance (chs. 2:23 to 3:6). In each

of these cases, he points to the fact that something new has
begun to happen, and old restrictions must be abandoned. Although these controversies may not actually have come to a
head until later in Jesus' ministry, they appear quite appropri-
ately at this point in Mark, since they demonstrate the radical
newness of Jesus' message and of the new age that God is
about to establish through him.

The Climax of the Galilean Ministry. At this stage in Jesus'
ministry, the popular response is at its peak. Jesus can scarcely
find time or place for solitude, and the crowds are coming
from Gentile regions outside the borders of Galilee (ch.
3:7-12). Efforts by Jesus to suppress Messianic claims made in
his behalf are unsuccessful and result rather in the furtherance
of his reputation. The circle of disciples is complete, and they
have been authorized to carry on the twofold ministry in
which he has been engaged: to preach the good news, and to
liberate men from the control of the evil powers (vs. 14-15).
From the scribes comes the charge that he is himself in league
with the demons. In answering the charge, Jesus discloses that
his mission involves nothing less than overcoming Satan and
stripping him of his resources (vs. 26-27).

More poignant than the opposition of officials is the re-
sistance to Jesus by his own family. In v. 21, " his friends " is
literally " those of him," and probably means his own family
(see v. 31). At this point in his career, therefore, his family is
so lacking in understanding of his mission that they think he
" is beside himself " (v. 21).

Mark breaks off the narrative to introduce the parables of
Jesus (ch. 4:1-34), which he treats as intentionally obscure
sayings of Jesus, designed to instruct the enlightened and confirm in their blindness those who cannot see (vs. 10-12). Actually, the parables seem to have been intended by Jesus to
provoke reflection, not to obscure the truth. Mark, or the com-

munity of Christians on whose resources he was drawing, adds to the parable of the sower a rather involved allegorical interpretation, which obscures its original encouragement to messengers of the gospel: " Your job is to sow; do not be discouraged by the fact that the response you get will be a mixed one."

The other parables and parabolic sayings point to various aspects of proclaiming the gospel: the message is to be announced, not guarded as a secret (ch. 4:21-25); the coming of the Kingdom is God's doing, once the message has been proclaimed (vs. 26-29); the Kingdom is now a reality in a way unobserved by mankind, but God will bring it to its designed consummation (vs. 30-32).

A string of vivid stories follow (chs. 4:35 to 5:43) which demonstrate the authority committed to Jesus as God's agent to establish his Kingdom. The stilling of the waves (ch. 5:35-41) points to God's sovereignty over nature; the colorful account of the Gerasene demoniac (ch. 5:1-20) reveals Jesus' authority over the demons; the healing of the woman with the flow of blood and the raising of Jairus' daughter (ch. 5:21-43) manifest Jesus' power over sickness and death.

One might suppose that such astounding acts as these would evoke faith, but the precise opposite is often the case, as we noted in a general way in Chapter 1. The people in his own home territory recognized that he had authority, but refused to believe that it was from God (Mark 6:1-6). They could not believe that a man whose origins and family and humble home life were known to them could be God's agent in their midst, and they became angrily hostile toward him. But in spite of the hostility, he sent out his disciples to carry on the work for which they had been chosen: to call men to repentance in view of the coming Kingdom and to serve as channels for God's overcoming the evil powers (vs. 7-13).

Beyond Galilee. In addition to the mounting opposition from his fellow countrymen, Jesus began to attract attention from the civil authorities, and specifically Herod Antipas, the son of Herod the Great, who had been appointed by the Romans as puppet governor of Galilee and Perea (the district east of the Jordan). The rumor had reached Herod that Jesus was John the Baptist raised from the dead. Although the story about John and Herod (vs. 14-20) has been made famous in art, literature, and music, its very familiarity obscures the fact that Herod was probably gravely concerned about Jesus as a potential Messianic pretender. His activities might stir up the people to revolt, thus bringing retribution by the Romans on Herod's territory. When word of John's fate reached Jesus, he took it as a signal to withdraw across the Lake of Galilee into country outside Herod's jurisdiction.

Before leaving to cross over into the Gentile territory on the eastern side of the lake, Jesus is said by Mark to have fed the crowd of five thousand. Explanations for this incident have ranged all the way from (1) the suggestion that the disciples found a cave filled with bread stored there by a local baker to (2) the more devout theory that each person had actually only a tiny fragment of food, but that in the joy of fellowship, each felt filled. Whatever the original event may have been, the story was told in the early church as a symbolic anticipation of the Lord's Supper, as is made explicit in the account of it given in the Gospel of John (ch. 6).

Mark tells us nothing of Jesus' activity in the Gentile region, except that en route Jesus appeared again as one having authority over nature (Mark 6:45-52). Various rational explanations have been offered for the story of Jesus' walking on the water. It was suggested that the lake of Galilee was quite shallow near the shore where Jesus was wading, and that a mist rising from the surface confused the disciples into thinking he was actually walking on the water. A more plausible explanation is that this is what scholars call an "epiphany story," coming from the early church, and told to support the claim that during Jesus' earthly ministry the glory of God was being revealed through his exercise of authority.

On his return to Galilee (chs. 6:53 to 7:23), the crowds sought him out again to be healed. And the religious leaders continued to harass him for his subversion of Jewish separateness and of their authority in reinterpreting the law of Moses. Another feeding is reported to have taken place, this time of four thousand and on Gentile soil. Probably this is another version of the feeding of five thousand. On his return to the Galilean side of the lake, the Pharisees came to him again with a request for a sign, but he, knowing that signs do not convince those who *will not* believe, refused to give one. By contrast, a man in the Gentile city of Bethsaida sought and was granted his sight (ch. 8:22-26).

The Messiahship Confessed. The turning point in the Gospel of Mark is the incident near Caesarea Philippi where Peter first publicly acknowledged Jesus as the Christ (vs. 27-29). But Peter did not yet understand what Messiahship involved for Jesus, who had to explain to his followers the role of suffering that he and all who would follow him must be prepared to accept. Mark records a divine attestation of Peter's confession in the story of the transfiguration of Jesus (ch. 9:2-8). But even then Jesus must stress the suffering allotted to the Messiah Son of Man.

The remaining chapters leading up to the Passion narrative underscore: (1) the power of Jesus over the evil spirits; (2) the status as servant that the disciple, like his master, must be prepared to accept; (3) Jesus' challenge to Jewish legalism. The section ends with a request by the disciples for places of special privilege in the Kingdom, sternly rebuked by Jesus, and with the last of Jesus' miracles, the healing of a blind man at Jericho (ch. 10:35-52).

The Ministry in Jerusalem. The entry of Jesus into Jerusalem symbolizes the way in which his vocation combines the authority of God's agent with the humility of God's servant (ch. 11:1-10). The authority is evident in the cleansing of the Temple (ch. 11:15-19). Jesus significantly quotes from Isa. 56:7, " My house shall be called a house of prayer *for all peoples,*" since the court designated as the spot where Gentiles could approach God had become a place of noise and commercial exploitation. The hostile reaction of the Jewish officials was intensified by his verbal attack on them. His challenge appears both in the allegory of the vineyard (Mark 12:1-12), in which they are made out to be the murderers of God's messengers, and in the series of sharp replies to questions addressed to him by the Pharisees and the aristocratic Sadducees (ch. 12:13-34). The atmosphere of hostility in these conflicts with the Jewish leaders has probably been intensified by the church because of Jewish-Christian antagonism at the time the Gospels were being written.

More fuel was added to the fires of official opposition to Jesus by his prediction of the destruction of the Temple (ch. 13:1-2), a statement which in garbled form was thrown up to him at his trial (ch. 14:58). In ch. 13, the early church has expanded his predictions about the coming end of the age, probably in view of the crises through which it was passing about the time Mark was being written. But, as we have noted, Jesus refused to set a definite time for the fulfillment of the promised Kingdom (v. 32).

THE PASSION AND THE RESURRECTION

From the time of Peter's confession of the Messiahship, Jesus had made repeated allusions to the fact that he expected soon to die. It seems likely that the early church expanded some of his references to his coming death into detailed prophecies of the crucifixion and the resurrection (Mark 8:31; 9:31; 10:33-34). It is, of course, possible that Jesus foresaw the specific details of his coming death, but it seems more likely that his original statements have been developed in the light of what actually occurred.

But even when we make allowances for the church's expansion of Jesus' words, there remains a series of indirect statements that point to his expectation of a violent death and an understanding of his death in the light of the Servant Songs of Second Isaiah (especially ch. 53). In verses such as Mark 9:12 and 10:45, the phrases " treated with contempt " and " for many " seem to be drawn from Second Isaiah, but their connection with either the circumstances of Jesus' death or the later church's interpretation of it is so indirect as to rule out the claim that these verses were produced by the early church. They sound like authentic words of Jesus. By linking together the Messiah Son of Man hopes of Israel with the Suffering Servant expectations of Second Isaiah, Jesus transformed the hopes of Judaism in the act of fulfilling them.

Up until the evening of the Last Supper, Jesus' references to his approaching death were veiled. In making explicit the announcement of his death, Jesus involved his disciples in an acted-out parable. The poured wine and the broken loaf symbolize the act of self-giving that Jesus was about to perform in submitting to death at the hands of the officials.

The last meal with the disciples is reported by Mark as a Passover celebration (ch. 14:12-25), although John 13:1 says that Jesus died before the night of the Passover. In the course of the meal, Jesus sought to interpret to the disciples the meaning of his act of laying down his life (" my blood "), of giving himself (" my body ") in their behalf. His death was to be the sacrifice that sealed the New Covenant (Mark 14:24), thus providing the basis for the creation of God's new people. Even in the face of death, he looked forward to the time to come in the future when God's purpose for and through his people would be fulfilled "in the kingdom of God" (v. 25).

There follows, in Mark 14:32-42, the familiar account of the struggle in the Garden, when even to the end, Jesus must decide for God's way to fulfill the Messianic role through suffering, rather than the popular, easy route to human success as a political victor.

Mark's account of the arrest, trial, and crucifixion is full of the vivid detail that suggests an eyewitness as one of his sources: the young man who fled naked from Gethsemane (ch. 14:51), the relationships of Simon of Cyrene who carried the cross of Jesus (ch. 15:21), the identity of Joseph of Arimathea who placed the body of Jesus in his own tomb (v. 43). But the resurrection story ends on a surprisingly inconclusive note. The tomb is empty, and Jesus' followers are instructed to go to Galilee where he will meet them. The women are silent and filled with fear, and the narrative breaks off in a grammatically awkward manner. Some scholars think that there was more in the original edition of Mark — perhaps an appearance of Jesus to Peter in Galilee (see ch. 16:7). But our oldest manuscripts end as the translation ends in the RSV: "For they were afraid."

One thing is certain: Mark believed that God raised Jesus from the dead. He quotes Jesus three times as saying he would rise again (chs. 8:31; 9:31; 10:34), and he would not have bothered writing his Gospel unless he had been convinced that God had done so. The Messiah, who was rejected and crucified by his own people, God has vindicated by raising from the dead. And that is the heart of the good news!

CHAPTER 4 | *The Gospel for the New People of God: Matthew*

MORE than any of the other Gospel writers, Matthew is eager to show the continuity and contrasts between God's ancient people, Israel, and his new people, the church. He is the only one who uses the word "church," but more important than that are his efforts to show how Jesus Christ is the fulfillment of the Hebrew Scriptures, how his new law fulfills the intent of the old. He even seems to have divided the main part of his book into five sections to resemble the five books of Moses, concluding each section with a statement summarizing Jesus' ministry (Matt. 7:28; 11:1; 13:53; 19:1; 26:1).

From the second century has come a tradition that Matthew, former tax collector and disciple of Jesus, wrote down in Hebrew the sayings of Jesus. On the supposition that the First Gospel was a Greek translation of this collection of Jesus' sayings, Matthew, the apostle, has been credited with its authorship. But there are several major difficulties with this conclusion, the most serious of which is the fact that the author has reproduced in slightly altered form nearly the whole of Mark, and has followed the Marcan sequence of events except where he wanted to improve the topical arrangement of his material. Usually he has been content merely to insert his additional material into Mark's structure without modifying the material

55

from Mark in any significant way. It seems unlikely that
Matthew, the disciple, who had been an eyewitness to Jesus'
life, would be so heavily dependent on Mark, who, so far as
we know, was not an eyewitness.

The author of Matthew was a man of paradoxical inclina-
tions. He is the most Jewish in outlook of the writers of the
Gospels, as is evident from his concern to present Jesus as the
giver of the new law. But he is also the most severely hostile
toward Jewish leaders and Jewish legalism. He alone reports
Jesus as having restricted the disciples to preaching the gospel
to Jews (Matt. 10:5-6), but he also quotes Jesus as declaring
that religious outcasts will take precedence over pious Jews in
the Kingdom of God (ch. 8:5-12). His attack on Jewish interpretation of the law is most radical, and yet he is careful to
report that Jesus said, " Till heaven and earth pass away, not
an iota, not a dot, will pass from the law until all is accomplished " (ch. 5:18). In spite of Matthew's shifting back and
forth between condemning Jewish legalism and promising fulfillment of its law, it is clear that he is profoundly concerned
about one major matter: the relationship between Judaism and
Christianity, between the old people of God and the new people of God. But before turning to an examination of Matthew's
understanding of the new people of God, we must survey
briefly the religious conditions among the Jews against which
both Jesus and the Gospel of Matthew raise their criticism.

Religious Groups Within Judaism

The Pharisees. The term " Pharisee " has come to be used
commonly for someone who professes moral or religious superiority. The Gospels tend to confirm this interpretation, but
that would be doing the Pharisees an injustice. They were in
many ways the real strength of first-century Judaism, though
numerically they were no more than a minority. The account

of them in the Gospels was written down at a time when mutual recrimination between Jew and Christian was the order of the day. Furthermore, what is said in the Gospels about the Pharisees does not seem to be applicable to the group as a whole, and certainly does not fit with their announced aims.

The name "Pharisee" probably comes from a word meaning "separate," and was used to point up the fact that those who called themselves God's people ought to separate themselves from the corruption of the world and live a pure life in obedience to God. A few scholars think, however, that the word comes from "Persian," and was applied to those Jews who incorporated into their faith ideas that were characteristic of the Persian religion: the belief in angels, in the resurrection, in paradise, in Satan.

The Pharisaic practice mentioned most frequently in the New Testament is that of reinterpreting the Old Testament. The reinterpretation was not developed as a means of evading the law; it was designed to demonstrate the contemporary vitality of God's ancient law. It corresponds to what preachers in our own time ought to be doing to interpret the Scripture. The Pharisees thought that the gift of prophecy had been supplanted by the gift of interpretation. God spoke in this day, they claimed, not through the prophets, but through the teachers who stood in the honored tradition stretching back (in theory, at least) to the day when the law had been given to Moses.

The Pharisees are sometimes spoken of as a "party." But, as a matter of fact, they took care to avoid political involvement with Rome. They believed that God would establish his Kingdom in his own time and by his own means. Their obligation was to obey his law and keep themselves from being corrupted by contact with the world.

The Scribes. The men assigned the task of interpretation of the law were called "scribes," and they developed the minute distinctions as to what was or was not permissible under the law. For example, the scribes debated whether or not one could eat an egg laid on the Sabbath, since the hen had to work on the Sabbath to produce it. Not all the scribal interpretations were so pedantic. A man could work on the Sabbath to break down a door if a child had been accidentally locked in a room. The interpretive work of the scribes was controlled by (1) sheer delight in the law and the endless possibilities of the interpreter's task; (2) the concern to show the relevance of the law to everyday living; and (3) the concern for human need.

But not all the scribes were motivated by such lofty goals. The cleverness of an interpretation became an end in itself. What started out as a commendable undertaking became the ground for religious pride and social aloofness. Against scribes and Pharisees of this variety Jesus' stinging condemnation was addressed. Those who should have been the channels of God's word for mankind became an offense by reason of their hypocrisy and disdain toward all others.

Sadducees and Essenes. One of the major points of disagreement between the Pharisees and their chief opponents, the Sadducees, was the question, What are the authoritative sacred books of Judaism? The Pharisees recognized not only the five books of Moses but the prophetical and historical writings as well, because they found there Scriptural grounds for their beliefs in the resurrection, Satan, etc. The Sadducees rejected these beliefs because they could not be documented in the Pentateuch. They were more liberal in social contacts and assumed positions of importance in the ruling council of the Jews to which Rome allowed a considerable degree of autonomy in local government. The Sadducees were largely from among the priestly and aristocratic families, so that their aloofness was an expression of snobbishness, not of piety.

As we observed in the preceding chapter, in spite of the discovery of the remarkable Essene library, which we know as the Dead Sea scrolls, there is no basis for associating Jesus with the Essenes. There are some striking common features between the New Testament and the scrolls, but these serve only to show us how widespread was the ferment within Judaism in Jesus' day and how much a man of his time Jesus was. (For a fuller treatment of the Jewish groups and their beliefs, see Lawrence E. Toombs, *The Threshold of Christianity*.)

Who Are the True People of God?

Where the Pharisees, Sadducees, and Essenes were concerned to create and preserve an exclusive group that would qualify for the right to be called the people of God, Jesus' whole mission was to proclaim that God welcomed into the fellowship of his people all who, recognizing their need for forgiveness, turned to him in grateful, obedient trust. His words were probably addressed originally to the masses of people who did not observe the religious ceremonies and ordinances, partly out of ignorance, perhaps in some cases out of economic necessity, but partly also because they found no satisfying religious significance in a religion of regulations. Jesus drew attention to this pointedly when he contrasted the response of Jewish officialdom to John the Baptist with their reaction to himself: " For John came neither eating nor drinking, and they say, ' He has a demon '; the Son of man came eating and drinking, and they say, ' Behold, a glutton and a drunkard, a friend of tax collectors and sinners! ' " (Matt. 11:18-19.)

But in the fulfillment of Old Testament prophecy Matthew sees the most important proof that the true people of God are those who recognize and acknowledge Jesus as Lord. The proofs from prophecy are especially common in the infancy narratives of Matthew (chs. 1 and 2), where the thesis is that the genealogy of Jesus, his birth of a virgin, its locale in Judea, the slaughter of the infants by Herod, the flight into Egypt, and the move to Nazareth demonstrate the link between Old Testament prophecies and the fulfillment God has given in Jesus Christ.

The argument from prophecy may seem to us today to be decidedly weak, since some of Matthew's quotations are given strained interpretations, and some cannot even be found in the Hebrew Scriptures. For example, " He shall be called a Nazarene " (Matt. 2:23) does not occur in any known Jewish source. Other quotations apply to situations different from the ones to which Matthew links them. The prophecy, " Out of Egypt have I called my son " (v. 15), is from Hos. 11:1, where it refers to the exodus from Egypt, but Matthew makes it apply to the flight into Egypt and subsequent return of the Holy Family. Two remarks may be in order about this practice. First, the interpretational *method* resembles that used by the Essenes, as attested by the discovery among the Dead Sea scrolls of commentaries on Old Testament books in which very similar liberties taken with the Scriptural text have been found.

The second observation is that the *intention* of this method is to demonstrate that God's purpose has not been thwarted by the Jews' failure to accept Jesus as the Christ, but is being fulfilled through the church. The pious folk of the first century believed that God's truth was not always manifest to the unworthy but could be discerned in its veiled form by those who had the needed spiritual insight to interpret the divinely inspired Scriptures. There is no hint in Matthew that the old revelation must be discarded; rather, it is to be transformed by being lifted up into a new sphere in which its meaning for

God's people will be realized fully. Hence the stress on, " This was done in order that it might be fulfilled . . ."

THE NEW LAW

Matthew was also interested in communicating to Christians the grounds for their ethical decisions as individuals and their common life as members of the church. The basic document for the ethical life is the section of Matthew we know as the Sermon on the Mount. Though we call it a " sermon," it is in fact a compact summary of the main themes of Jesus' teaching on many occasions. Luke includes some of the material found in Matthew's Sermon on the Mount, but he has scattered it throughout his Gospel and reports Jesus' words as being spoken under very different circumstances. This selection and rearrangement (of material drawn from the Sayings Source, Q) suggests that the Sermon as we now have it is Matthew's arrangement, not a verbatim report of what Jesus said on one particular occasion. But Matthew scores a dramatic point by describing Jesus as giving the new law on a mountain in Galilee just as Moses gave the old law on a mountain in Sinai.

The Sermon opens in Matthew with the familiar Beatitudes, which appear here (Matt. 5:3-12) in a full form that contrasts sharply with the simpler version that Luke gives. Luke quotes Jesus as saying, for example, " Blessed are *you* poor " (Luke 6:20), a direct address to the present state of the poor. But Matthew's version changes the statement into a general principle with a more religious connotation: " Blessed are *the* poor in spirit " (Matt. 5:3). Similarly, Luke's declaration of the blessedness of the hungry is modified to " those who hunger and thirst for righteousness."

Because of these so-called spiritualizing tendencies of Matthew, some interpreters have concluded that this Gospel is

mainly concerned with the inner spiritual state of the individual Christian. But the Beatitudes are words of encouragement
and assurance to those who are awaiting the coming of God's
Kingdom. The righteousness spoken of by Matthew (chs. 5:6,
10; 6:33) may refer to man's seeking to gain a righteous inner
condition, but it may also be used in the Old Testament sense
of God's righteousness, that is, his activity in the world, seeking to restore it to obedience to his will. If the latter interpretation is correct, then " hungering for God's righteousness "
would correspond to the expectation expressed in the familiar
words of the Lord's Prayer:

> " Thy kingdom come,
>   Thy will be done,
>   On earth as it is in heaven."
>   (Matt. 6:10.)

Jesus' ethic centers in God. It is he who rewards man's acts
of mercy. It is he who forgives man, and thereby lays on man
the obligation to forgive his fellow man. Loving our enemies is
more than a moral obligation; it is a demand placed upon
us because God is our Father, and having created us in his
image he expects us to display the characteristics of our Father
(ch. 5:44). Put in its most striking form, the injunction stands:
" You, therefore, must be perfect, *as your heavenly Father is
perfect"* (ch. 5:48). The Hebrew term that lies behind the
word translated " perfect " means " whole," " complete," " at
peace." The point is that as God is complete in his nature and
in the fulfillment of his purposes, so a man should seek to be
completely what God intended him to be in creating him.

Because Jesus grounds his ethical demand in the nature of
God, he does not offer any universally applicable rules for
living. Rather, the more Jesus teaches his followers about
God — his active love, his concern to reconcile the estranged,
his will to forgive the sinner, his purpose to liberate the en-

slaved — the greater is the obligation upon them to respond by manifesting these characteristics in their dealings with their fellow men: "Forgive us our debts, as we also have forgiven our debtors" (Matt. 6:12). Jesus' ethic in the Sermon on the Mount is not a set of abstract moral principles which he sets forth as man's obligation, but it is the call to obey the living God who is showing his love to man in the ministry and message of his anointed Son.

This is the basis of Jesus' words on prayer (vs. 5-8), on freedom from anxiety (vs. 25-34), on judging (ch. 7:1-5), on treasures (ch. 6:19-21). Because God has dealt with man in such a gracious and dependable way, he ought so to deal with the persons that he encounters. The new law is not a law at all in the ordinary sense; it is the announcement of a new basis for man's relationship to God. In response to God's nature as thus revealed, the relationships of man to life, to death, and to his fellow man are transformed.

Matthew also records that Jesus gave a sharp critique of the old law. This section (ch. 5:17-48) is familiar from the repeated phrases, "You have heard that it was said to the men of old . . . but I say to you . . ." In each case, Matthew reports a law of the Jews accepted as authoritative, and then sets Jesus' ethical requirement over against it. In some cases Jesus' alternative is a change from outward act (e.g., murder) to inner intent (hatred). In others, Jesus flatly rejects a practice allowable under Jewish law: for example, retaliation for injury (vs. 38-39), or swearing (vs. 33-37).

In spite of Jesus' direct way of dismissing the laws and interpretations hallowed by centuries, he did not intend to destroy the law of Moses: "I have come not to abolish . . . [the Law and the Prophets] but to fulfil them" (v. 17). "Fulfil" does not mean to do what the Law and the Prophets had predicted the Messiah would do, but, as the contrast with "abolish " shows, it means to display the fullness of meaning intended by God in giving the law to his people. Jesus' quarrel is not so much with the law as with the misuse to which it had been put. The law was given, not as the basis for pride in the Jew's religious superiority, but to remind men of their responsibility to obey God if they were to be called his people.

At the same time, we can see how Matthew himself has on occasion fallen into the trap of trying to convert Jesus' ethic into a set of rules. For example, in Mark, Jesus is recorded as rejecting without any qualification the possibility of a man's divorcing his wife and marrying another (Mark 10:11). But Matthew betrays a tendency to calculate the circumstances under which an exception might be made: if the wife is unfaithful (" on the ground of unchastity "), the husband may divorce her and remarry (Matt. 5:32; 19:9). Although Matthew is eager to strike out against legalism within Judaism, he is unable to detach himself wholly from it even in transmitting the teachings of Jesus.

How Shall the Church Regulate Its Life?

The only places in any of the Gospels where the word " church " appears are in Matt. 16:18 and 18:17. Although there is fairly general agreement that ch. 18 assumed its present form in the light of needs of the church, scholars do not agree about the authenticity of these words ascribed to Jesus. Some say flatly, " Jesus never intended to found the church, so he could not have spoken these words." Some Protestant scholars, troubled by the way the Roman Church has used ch. 16:18 to support its claims for the authority of the pope, have rejected the authenticity of the verse. But the verses can be accepted as authentic words of Jesus without drawing from them the conclusions drawn by Roman Catholics.

There is nothing inherently improbable in assuming that

Jesus spoke of gathering a community of the faithful who were awaiting the coming of God's Kingdom. As a matter of fact, if he made Messianic claims for himself, it would be surprising for him *not* to have spoken of a circle of followers who shared his expectations. It is more likely that Jesus anticipated the formation of a " church," with the disciples as its nucleus, than that he laid down rules to govern its life. On this ground, the probability that Matt. 16:18 is authentic is stronger than that ch. 18:17 may be. The fact that the words in ch. 16:18 are found only in Matthew simply points up the possibility that only this Gospel preserves a genuine saying that was otherwise unknown.

For Jesus to have called Simon Bar-Jona "this rock" may have seemed ironic, especially in the closing hours of Jesus' life when Simon denied his Lord. But Peter was the spokesman for the disciples. He first enunciated the faith in Jesus as Messiah. To him, Jesus first appeared risen from the dead, as we learn by inference from Mark (ch. 16:7) and by Paul's explicit statement (I Cor. 15:5). Peter as the first witness of the risen Christ is in a real sense the rock on which Christ built his church. And Matt. 16:18 points to the fact that, of the one generation of believers who saw with their own eyes Jesus Christ risen from the dead, Simon Peter was the first in time and in importance.

Apart from the question of the authenticity of these references, Matthew shows that by the time he was writing there was need for authority in settling disputes within the church itself. Controversies between members were to be settled privately, but if the disputing parties refused to accept a settlement, the issue was to be brought before the whole congregation (ch. 18:15-17), which could expel a member (v. 17). In ch. 18, Matthew has brought together words of Jesus that he felt to be important for the inner life of the Christian com-

munity: on forgiveness (vs. 21-35); on humility (vs. 3-4); on the necessity for self-denial (vs. 7-9). The words of v. 35 sound as though they might have been added by someone who wanted to make even forgiveness a legal obligation. In such a solemn context, Matthew has placed these words of Jesus about how Christians ought to get along with each other.

MEMBERSHIP IN GOD'S PEOPLE

At the outset of Jesus' ministry, Matthew reports him as instructing the disciples to go only " to the lost sheep of the house of Israel " (ch. 10:6). At the end of his career (in chs. 19 to 27), Jesus implies in parables and instructions that repentant sinners will have priority over religious leaders. The repeated phrase " the first shall be last " points to the conviction that those who think they have priority with God will find themselves in last place in the day of consummation.

This is the point in Matthew's story of the young man who takes pride in his moral superiority and has confidence in his wealth (ch. 19:16-30). After the man has left, Jesus promises the disciples that they will have a central role in the Day of Judgment (v. 28), whereas the aristocratic and religiously acceptable will fall under judgment.

The same theme appears in the parable of the laborers in the vineyard (Matt. 20:1-16). Those who think they have a prior claim on God and his rewards find themselves no better off than the rest. Originally this parable probably focused on the generosity of God (v. 15) and the resentment of those who insist on legalistic ideas of rewards and punishments. In Matthew's version it becomes a rebuke of the peevish religious leaders who will take last place (v. 16) after the latecomers.

Matthew, Mark, and Luke all record the parable of the wicked tenants, but Matthew outdoes the rest in attacking the Jews for their unbelief (Matt. 21:33-46). He alludes to the

Jewish leaders who plotted Jesus' death as "those wretches" (v. 41). He repeats twice that the vineyard (an Old Testament figure for the people of God, as in Isa., ch. 5) and later "the kingdom of God" will be taken from them and given to others (Matt. 21:41, 43). So that no one can miss the force of this threat, Matthew adds: "When the chief priests and the Pharisees heard his parables, they perceived that he was speaking about them" (v. 45).

In the parable of the wedding feast, Matthew records Jesus as saying that those who had first been invited killed the king's servants (ch. 22:6). Obviously interpreting the destruction of Jerusalem as a divine judgment on Judaism, he reports that "the king [God] was angry, and he sent his troops and destroyed those murderers and burned their city" (v. 7). We cannot doubt Matthew's conviction that the Jews have forfeited their exclusive claim to being the people of God.

Only in Matthew's version of Jesus' great discourse about the end of the age (chs. 24 and 25) do we find the account of the Last Judgment (ch. 25:31-46), which shows that Jesus' mission is not confined to Judaism or even to the church, but includes "the nations" (v. 32). The Judge decides who may or may not enter the Kingdom of God by the acts of mercy that have been done toward the hungry, the homeless, the imprisoned. Without their realizing the consequences of their acts, many will be vindicated in the Day of Judgment because they have shown mercy, and others will stand condemned because they have not. The element of surprise increases the drama of this story (which is not meant as a literal description of the Judgment Day), since neither the just nor the unjust know their fate in advance. Those condemned prided themselves on their religiosity, and yet failed to show mercy to others as God had shown mercy to them; those adjudged righteous acted compassionately, simply because they saw their fellow men in distress, and expected nothing in return. The whole ground of justification before God by conformity to ritual or by guarding oneself from moral contamination is undercut. And because it is, the Gentile nations share in the rewards meted out at the Last Judgment.

To point up the unbelief of the Jewish officials, Matthew alone has reported the request of "the chief priests and the Pharisees" to Pilate for a guard at the tomb of Jesus to prevent his disciples from stealing the body and claiming that he has risen from the dead (ch. 27:62-66). The sequel to the story — also found only here — is that after Jesus was raised from the dead, the officials bribed the soldiers to say that the disciples had stolen the body (ch. 28:11-15).

"Go . . . Make Disciples of All Nations"

The Gospel of Matthew ends on the strongest note of universal outreach of any of the Gospels. Having been rejected and crucified on the holy mountain of the Jews in Jerusalem, Jesus stands on a mountain in "Galilee of the Gentiles" (ch. 4:15) and commands his disciples to go to all nations under his authority, preaching, teaching, and baptizing in his name (ch. 28:19; the phrase "Father . . . Son and . . . Holy Spirit" is probably an echo of the baptismal formula of the early church rather than an actual quotation from Jesus). And finally, he promises to be with them until the establishing of the Kingdom and the summoning of the new people of God are accomplished, and the present age comes to its consummation (ch. 28:20).

CHAPTER 5 | *The Gospel for Humanity: Luke*

The word "humanity" can mean either "the human race" or "concern for others as human beings." In Luke's Gospel both aspects of humanity are of major importance. In a manner that is free of the anti-Jewish polemic of Matthew, Luke shows that the gospel is for all men, for Gentiles as well as for Jews. To Luke we are indebted for those records of Jesus' teaching which stress more than the others the love of God for the needy and the corresponding love that God's children should display. Before tracing this theme through the Gospel, let us look at a question that may strike the thoughtful reader when he considers Luke's opening verses (ch. 1:1-4): How sound is Luke's claim to have written an orderly account of Jesus based on the testimony of eyewitnesses? What is Luke's worth as a historian?

LUKE AS A HISTORIAN

Luke writes in the style characteristic of Greek historians of the early Roman period. This impression is confirmed by Luke's frequent references to rulers and public officials, to geographical detail, and by his effort to associate the events of the gospel narrative with contemporary events in the Roman world. Notice, for example, chs. 1:5, 2:1, and especially 3:1-3, where the emperor, the governors, the petty monarchs of the region, and the incumbent high priests are all mentioned by name.

As we observed in Chapter 1, the writers of the Gospels are interested in communicating the gospel, not in objective accounts of Jesus. Luke does give the impression, however, of one who has recorded faithfully and accurately the tradition as it came to him. At many points, he preserves a more original form of a saying of Jesus'. For example, the phrase " finger of God " (Luke 11:20) is almost certainly the expression Jesus used rather than " Spirit of God," which appears in Matthew. Similarly, the parables in Luke are more nearly free of interpretive additions than Matthew's, as may be observed by comparing the parable of the marriage feast (Matt. 22:1-14) with the parable of the banquet (Luke 14:16-24). At the same time, Luke feels free to reorganize his material in order to make it support the picture of Jesus' life and ministry that he is developing. His arrangement of the material is "orderly" (ch. 1:3), even though it may not be in strict chronological order.

Luke gives further evidence of his contact with the events of his own time by occasional references to historical developments in Palestine, such as Pilate's slaughter of some Galileans (ch. 13:1-9). There is an indirect reference to the siege of Jerusalem by the Roman Armies (which took place a generation after Jesus' crucifixion) in ch. 21:20. By the fact that he went beyond the story of Jesus' ministry to write a second volume, the book of The Acts, Luke showed that the story of God's purpose would not be complete until the gospel had penetrated to the Gentile nations (in The Acts it reaches Rome).

In addition to the two sources used in common with Matthew (Mark and Q, the Sayings Source) Luke had a rich source of his own that included several distinctive parables and such colorful incidents as the encounter of Jesus with Zacchaeus, the tax collector (ch. 19:1-10). His version of the words of Jesus at the Last Supper (ch. 22:15-22, as one group of manuscripts preserves them) is strikingly different from the form found in Mark and Matthew. Luke does not mention the blood of the covenant, as the other writers do. And the passing of the cup comes before the breaking of bread. The cup in Luke's version is an anticipation of the wine that will be shared in the heavenly banquet, a familiar Jewish figure for the life of fellowship in the new age. Although this raises difficulties for historians seeking to reconstruct the original form of the Lord's Supper, the fact that Luke records it in this form testifies to his concern to report the traditions as they came to him. It is possible that Luke has preserved a tradition of the Lord's Supper as it was known and practiced in some particular region of the early church, showing that the Communion practice was not uniform throughout the church.

GOOD NEWS TO THE POOR

In Luke's Gospel, Jesus has not yet appeared on the scene when the theme sounds that the gospel is for the poor, the religious outcasts, the socially unacceptable. In Mary's song (often called " The Magnificat "), the expectant mother sings of the God who is sending her the still unborn child:

> " He has put down the mighty from their thrones,
>   and exalted those of low degree;
> he has filled the hungry with good things,
>   and the rich he has sent empty away."

(Luke 1:52-53.)

The aged Simeon praises God for sending his good news *to all people:*

> " Lord, now lettest thou thy servant depart in peace,
>   according to thy word;

for mine eyes have seen thy salvation
which thou hast prepared in the presence of *all peoples,*
a light for revelation *to the Gentiles,*
and for glory to thy people Israel."

(Ch. 2:29-32.)

In introducing the story of John the Baptist, all four writers of the Gospels quote the familiar words from Isa., ch. 40:

" The voice of one crying in the wilderness:
Prepare the way of the Lord,
make his paths straight."

Only Luke continues the quotation to include the words, " and all flesh [that is, all humanity] shall see the salvation of God " (ch. 3:6). But the words that sound the major theme of the gospel are found in Jesus' selection of Scripture when he is invited to speak in the synagogue at Nazareth (ch. 4:16-19):

" The Spirit of the Lord is upon me,
because he has anointed me *to preach good news
to the poor.*"

In the address that follows, Jesus points out that, in the Old Testament, God's special concern was for the needy who stood outside the Hebrew faith, like Naaman, the Syrian, and the widow from Sidon.

In Luke's version of the Sermon (according to ch. 6:17, it was delivered on a level place rather than on a mountain), Jesus emphasizes that those who are poor in God's sight and who know their need will receive his blessing, " Blessed are you poor, for yours is the kingdom of God " (ch. 6:20). Conversely, woes are pronounced on the rich, the self-satisfied. Jesus answers the friends of John the Baptist, who came to ask about his Messianic role, in the same way, " Go and tell John what you have seen and heard: . . . *the poor have good news preached to them* " (ch. 7:22).

The word " poor " is used by Luke to include social and

religious outcasts, the spiritually deprived Gentiles, and those literally poor (therefore judged by Jewish piety to be under divine disfavor). Luke's interest extends also to women, who had few privileges in the social or religious life of first-century Judaism. For each of these types of persons, Jesus brought good news.

The Good News for Gentiles. Luke reports (ch. 9:1 ff.) that Jesus gave his disciples authority to carry on his work of overcoming the evil powers and preaching the good news of the Kingdom. A more important place is given in Luke's Gospel to the sending of seventy followers to engage in a ministry of itinerant preaching (ch. 10:1-16). It is recorded (v. 17) that these messengers met with great success in overcoming the demonic powers, a sign to Jesus that the final doom of Satan is now sealed. The number seventy (in some manuscripts, seventy-two) was believed by Jews of that period to be the number of the nations on earth. Accordingly, these traveling preachers symbolize the mission of the nations, as contrasted with the Twelve who went out on the mission to Israel (the nation of twelve tribes). The success of the Seventy is a token of the receptivity of the Gentiles to the good news.

At several points in the Gospels, an issue is raised with Jesus about *signs*. The Jewish leaders want Jesus to perform some spectacular act in order to prove to them that he has God's authorization for his ministry. Luke gives an account of one such conflict over the question of signs (ch. 11:29-32), in which Jesus surprisingly uses Gentiles as his examples of those who believed when they saw signs from God. The men of heathen Nineveh responded in faith to the preaching of Jonah; the Queen of Sheba was eager to hear the wisdom of Solomon. The implication is that the Israelites, who should have been concerned, were not, whereas *the Gentiles* responded in faith.

The Good News for the Deprived. Several parables in Luke

develop the theme of good news to the poor by demonstrating
the reversal of fortunes in the age to come. The two most familiar parables in this connection are the rich man and Lazarus (ch. 16:19-31), and the Pharisee and the publican (ch.
18:9-14). The one deals with literal poverty; the second treats
of spiritual poverty in the man who knows his sinfulness and
confesses his failure to obey God. The " poor " one in each case
is the man who is justified. The story of Lazarus is told in
terms of the concept of heaven and hell widely held among
Jesus' contemporaries, but it ought not to be taken as a literal
picture of life in the age to come. The point of the story is that
the man who has all he needs in this life, but has no concern
for the needy around him, finds himself in desperate need in
the life to come. And the poor wretch who is deprived of every
comfort and all security in this life is blessed in the age to
come. What could be better news for the poor than this?

The Good News for Sinners. The more profound of the two
stories is that of the Pharisee and the publican. The Pharisee
who is confident of his worth in the sight of God is given no
promise of justification, but the man who penitently acknowl-
edges his sin and depends only on God's mercy goes forth
justified before God. The message of this story is the same as
that of the parables in ch. 15 of Luke, all of which are filled
with rejoicing over the recovery of the lost: the return of the
lost sheep; the finding of a lost coin; the restoration to fellowship of the errant son. Significantly, the parable of the prodigal
son (Luke 15:11-32) ends with the complaint of the elder son
who stayed home — the one who supposed he had a place of
special privilege in the eyes of the father. The point of these
parables of joy is made in ch. 15:10: " Even so, I tell you, there
is joy before the angels of God [i.e., God himself rejoices] over
one sinner who repents."

The Good News for Women. In the Semitic world of Jesus'

day, women had few rights and almost no opportunities outside of rearing children and caring for a home. They were required to sit in a balcony at synagogue services and could not
enter the inner court of the Temple. But throughout his Gospel, Luke displays a special concern for women. The central
figures in the Nativity stories, apart from the children, are the
two mothers, Elizabeth and Mary. Luke alone records the
stories of Jesus' healing the son of the widow at Nain (ch.
7:11-15), of the anointing of Jesus by a woman at the house of
a Pharisee (ch. 7:36-50), of the financial support provided by
women for Jesus' ministry (ch. 8:1-3), of Mary and Martha
(ch. 10:38-42), of the crippled woman healed on the Sabbath
(ch. 13:10-17), of the woman who lost a coin (ch. 15:8-10), of
the women who weep as Jesus goes to Golgotha (ch. 23:27-30),
of the details of the women's report to the disciples that the
tomb is empty (ch. 24:10-11). The central role that women
play in Luke (the same is true of The Acts) reminds us of the
strategic place of women in the early church as supporters, as
witnesses, as pillars of faith.

LUKE'S SPECIAL STORIES AND SAYINGS

Among the sayings and stories found only in Luke are some
of the best-loved parts of the New Testament, and some of the
most difficult. In the former category is the parable of the good
Samaritan (ch. 10:29-37). As is well known, the Samaritans
were thought by the Jews to be a mixed breed, and therefore
were regarded as even more objectionable than if they had
been pure-blooded Gentiles. The great irony of Jesus' story is
that a despised Samaritan proves to be neighbor by ministering
to the robber's victim, while the Jewish leaders, the priest and
the Levite, pass him by. Attempts have been made to allegorize
this parable (that is, to find symbolic significance in each
detail of the story), but only one main point is made: the man

who fulfills the command to love his neighbor acts in mercy and compassion toward anyone he encounters who is in need. Equally clear is the parable of the rich fool (ch. 12:13-20), who places false confidence in the power of his possessions to sustain his life and provide him with security. When his life ends, his wealth is left behind and is no longer of any use to him whatsoever.

Among the difficult sayings of Jesus recorded by Luke are the parables of the friend at midnight (ch. 11:5-8), the unjust steward (ch. 16:1-13), and the unjust judge (ch. 18:1-8). Each of these sounds on first reading as though some unworthy action were being commended by Jesus or some unworthy characteristic being ascribed to God. The clue to keep in mind is that parables usually have only one point to make. To try to draw moral lessons from details of the story is to risk distorting the intended meaning. With this view in mind, the following major meanings emerge from these difficult parables: (1) If a *man* is willing to rouse his family in order to comply with the insistent request of a neighbor, how much more will *God* hear and answer those who ask him? (2) Jesus' hearers, who must face up to the crisis of the coming end of the age, will do well to act decisively and prudently (though not dishonestly) in anticipation of it. (3) If an irresponsible and unjust judge will hear a persistent woman and act, how much more will God, who listens patiently when his people cry day and night (ch. 18:7)?

The Real Meaning of Christian Fellowship

One of the most beautiful phrases that Jesus uses to describe his followers is " little flock " (Luke 12:32). Jesus' promise that God will give the Kingdom to the " little flock " is echoed in the words addressed to the disciples at the Lord's Supper (ch. 22:28-30). Because his followers have continued with him in spite of trials, God has appointed for them a share in the life of the Kingdom that is coming. When Jesus says, "So do I appoint for you," we could translate, "So do I covenant with you," a reference to the covenant through which the Kingdom is established. The followers of Jesus are the nucleus of the new people. They will "sit at table" (a symbol of the fullness of their joyous fellowship), and they will sit "on thrones judging the twelve tribes of Israel" (a symbol of their share in God's work of establishing his righteous rule over his creation).

But the fellowship of which Luke writes is not to be confined merely to the age to come; it is a possibility for the people of faith here and now (ch. 24:13-35). In the vivid story of Jesus' appearance to the two disciples on the road to Emmaus we have a symbolic picture of the way in which the risen Lord comes — often unknown and unrecognized — to his followers. The disciples are despondent because the nation has not been "redeemed"; that is, its nationalistic hopes have not been achieved (v. 21). Even the testimony of the women that the tomb was empty failed to convince them. The insurmountable obstacle for them was that they could not think of a suffering Messiah, and it is precisely this truth that the unrecognized Lord seeks to establish by appeal to the prophets.

But insight into Jesus' identity comes, not during the time of instruction, but in the time of fellowship: "He was known to them in the breaking of the bread" (Luke 24:35). The supreme moment in which the risen Christ is made known to his people is when they are sharing with him in the Communion. The Lord's Supper was then — and ought to be now — an experience of his presence with his followers: "He took the bread and blessed [God], and broke it, and gave it to them. And their eyes were opened and they recognized him" (vs. 30-31).

The meaning of fellowship involves God's people also in on-going responsibility. The call to repentance and the announcement of God's forgiveness are to be continued by Jesus' followers. To enable them to fulfill the ministry committed to them, God will send a special endowment of power (ch. 24:49), which the book of The Acts reveals to be the coming of the Holy Spirit (Acts, chs. 1 and 2). Luke's theme of the gospel for humanity carries through to the close of the book; the message of repentance and forgiveness is to be preached *to all nations,* although it begins at Jerusalem where the sacrifice of Jesus Christ took place.

For Luke, therefore, the " new people " begins where the " old people " came to an end. A verse of obscure meaning, recorded in both Matthew and Luke (Matt. 11:12; Luke 16:16) is used by Luke to underscore the universality of the gospel: " The law and the prophets were until John; since then the good news of the kingdom of God is preached, and every one enters it violently." In Matthew's version, the point is that the Kingdom is overcoming the powers that oppose it and is manifesting its own power. But, as Luke shows, to enter the Kingdom is no mild matter; it demands determination, forth-right action, willingness to engage in conflict or to suffer. The new situation has arrived. The days of the Law and the Prophets ended with John, and with the passing of that era went the possibility of a casual attitude toward God. Now those who aspire to be his people must " exercise force " or " enter the kingdom violently." But the invitation to participate in this struggle in behalf of the coming of God's Kingdom is no longer restricted. The possibility for fellowship, for hope, for worship, for sharing in the ministry, for struggle, is open to everyone.

| *The Gospel of Eternity: John*

THERE has been a great flurry of recent interest in the Gospel of John because the Dead Sea scrolls allegedly provide evidence concerning its age and authorship. The scrolls, which date from before the birth of Christ, contain material that resembles some of the terms and perspectives found in the Gospel of John. This fact has led a few scholars, and a great many interested laymen, to the conclusion that John must be the oldest of the Gospels. It is very important to know that some of the points of view in John's Gospel were held by Jews in Palestine before the birth of Jesus, since previously it had been thought that such views could be found only in places outside Palestine, such as Alexandria. But the Dead Sea scrolls do not tell us when or where the Gospel of John was written. The smooth, simple Greek in which it is written suggests that the early fathers of the church were right in their belief that it was written in a Greek-speaking land like Asia Minor.

There are some striking differences in *content* between John and the other three Gospels: (1) John has little interest in Jesus' ministry in Galilee, and describes mostly incidents in Jerusalem or Judea; (2) many of the incidents narrated do not come to any conclusion, but serve chiefly as introductions to long discourses on theological themes. For example, the familiar interview between Jesus and Nicodemus (John, ch.3) slips over from a dialogue between them to a statement about eternal life.

In addition, there are many differences of *detail* between John and the other Gospels. In John, Jesus meets John the Baptist but is not baptized. The cleansing of the Temple takes place at the beginning of Jesus' ministry rather than at the end. John, in contradiction to the other Gospels, states that the Last Supper was not a Passover meal. In the first three Gospels, Jesus' Messiahship is mentioned only indirectly or privately, but in John it is public and explicit.

On the other hand, John includes some important historical information that would not otherwise be available. His Gospel tells about apparent conflict between the followers of John the Baptist and those of Jesus (chs. 3:22 to 4:3). He alone indicates that Jesus died on the eve of the Passover, rather than on the afternoon following the Passover, as the other Gospels report. If John is correct on this point, it would be additional evidence that he is interested in some of the historical details of what happened in Jesus' ministry. But his chief concern is to communicate the meaning for faith of Jesus Christ, the Word of God "made flesh." Accordingly, we look to John's Gospel for the theological meaning of Jesus, not for verbatim reports of his teachings or objective accounts of his work.

Was this unnamed writer of the Fourth Gospel one of the original followers of Jesus, and therefore an eyewitness of the events he describes? We cannot flatly exclude this possibility, but the book itself presents no clear evidence that he was. On the contrary, the preoccupation of the writer with events in Jerusalem, rather than in the region of Galilee from which Jesus' original followers came, suggests that the author (or the one who preserved the traditions) was not one of the Twelve. In John 18:16 and 19:27, we learn that " the beloved disciple "

— who is presumably the author of the book or the source of its traditions — was known to the high priest and lived in Jerusalem, an unlikely possibility for a Galilean fisherman. Perhaps toward the end of his ministry Jesus drew to his circle of followers a young man from Jerusalem who in old age wrote the Gospel or preserved the traditions it draws upon. Although the early church reports that an aged leader of the church by the name of John lived in Ephesus and wrote the Fourth Gospel toward the end of the first century, we have no way of knowing whether he was one of the disciples. But the important consideration is that, whether eyewitness or not — and the likelihood is that he was not — the writer is more interested in the inner meaning of what Jesus said, and makes no attempt to reproduce Jesus' actual words.

THE TIME IS NOW

More subtle than the differences in content between John and the other Gospels is the difference in perspective on the coming of God's Kingdom. In each of the other Gospels there is some definite word about the time when God will consummate his purposes for the world and establish his Kingdom. On occasion the other Gospel writers deny that anyone can predict the time of fulfillment, and yet they mention specific pointers by which it can be known in advance. " There are some standing here who will not taste death before they see the kingdom of God come with power." (Mark 9:1.) " And this gospel of the kingdom will be preached throughout the whole world . . . and then the end will come." (Matt. 24:14.)

It is quite different in John. The writer conveys to us the sense that the day of consummation has already begun. Eternal life is not merely to be bestowed upon the faithful on the Day of Judgment; it is a present possibility, which man may enter

in every moment of faith (John 3:36). The judgment is not
simply a future event; it takes place whenever man decides
either for or against the will of God, and thereby " has eternal
life " or is excluded from it (ch. 5:24). The Kingdom of God
is a present reality into which man may enter now (ch. 3:3, 5).
The resurrection is an experience into which men of faith have
already entered in this life (ch. 5:25). The effect of all this is
to transform the urgency of the gospel message. There is no
longer an atmosphere of an impending judgment or consummation, since the benefits of the day of consummation are already accessible to faith in the here-and-now. The urgency
lies in the inescapable fact that man must decide in every moment for or against the will of God.

John has not, however, eliminated all sense of a fulfillment
in the future. There are repeated references in ch. 6 to the
resurrection " at the last day." Explicit mention is made in ch.
5:28-29 of the future resurrection and judgment. Although
interpretations of ch. 14:3 vary widely, it appears to be a promise of a future coming of Christ to his own people. Yet the
weight of emphasis falls on the present possibilities for enter-
ing the resurrection life and the joys of the Kingdom.

THE ETERNAL WORD

John's changed perspective on time affects not only his understanding of the future but also his outlook on the past. Just
as the fulfillment of the Christian's hope has a timeless quality,
so also the appearance of Jesus Christ is really a disclosure *in
time* of an eternal purpose: the Word of God (ch. 1:1). The
Greek word *logos,* usually translated " word," actually has far
richer significance than this translation suggests. The basic
meaning comes from the Old Testament idea of the word of
the Lord (for example, in Isa. 55:10-11), which is the declared
purpose of God to create the world and to bring it into sub-

jection to his will. The theme is sounded in the opening verses of Genesis, "And God said . . . and it was so." For God to speak is for him to announce his purpose; and for him to state his purpose is to guarantee its fulfillment. The " word," therefore, is far more than something God says; it is also what he does in order to fulfill his purpose.

When John describes Jesus as " the Word become flesh," he refers both to what Jesus said by way of making known God's will and to what he did in order to liberate men from bondage to sickness, sin, and death. But the Word made flesh includes also who Jesus is as a person in his relationships to other persons and in the authority that is manifest through him. Although the Word is mentioned explicitly only in John 1:1-18, it provides the main fabric of the entire Gospel. We shall trace this theme as it appears in three main aspects: (1) the " signs " Jesus performs (ch. 20:30-31); (2) the "I am" sayings throughout the book; (3) the meaning of Christ unfolded in the discourses. In the concluding parts of this chapter we shall note what John means when he says, " The Word was God " (ch. 1:1). And finally, we shall see how the work begun by the Word made flesh in Jesus Christ is continued by God's Spirit operating through his people.

SIGNS THAT GOD IS AT WORK

Because of the statement in John 20:31 that the writer has set down " these signs " in order that his readers might believe Jesus is the Christ, many interpreters have inferred that the signs were intended to be proofs of Jesus' Messiahship. Actually, a sign is not a " proof " at all. The clue to understanding the purpose of the signs is given by John himself in ch. 2:11, where it is said that the first of Jesus' signs (changing water into wine) " manifested his glory," and that, as a result, the disciples believed in him. Does John mean that the signs create faith? Actually, he says that only the disciples, not anyone else, believed after the sign at Cana. The signs are given, not to generate faith or to command it by some inescapable logic, but to illuminate and enrich it. The disciples already have faith, but each of Jesus' signs or symbolic acts brings a further unfolding of what God intends to do for his people. Miracles do not convert the unbelievers; their message is for those who already trust God.

There is no clear agreement among interpreters as to how many incidents John intended to be considered as " signs." Possibly he meant to include only seven, which was a sacred number among the Jews. Two of them are specifically listed as first (ch. 2:11) and second (ch. 4:54), but perhaps another has been added between these two: the cleansing of the Temple (ch. 2:13-22). The other signs include the healing of the paralytic (ch. 5:1-18), the feeding of the five thousand (ch. 6:4-14), and the raising of Lazarus (ch. 11:1-44). Possibly the story of Jesus' walking on the water should also be added (ch. 6:16-25). Behind the outward form of each story lies a symbolic meaning in which the nature of God and his purpose for his people are revealed.

The changing of water into wine takes place significantly at a wedding feast, a favorite Jewish symbol of the time of fellowship that God's people would enjoy in the new age. But in this story the Jewish provisions are inadequate (ch. 2:3, 6) either to bring joy or to effect purification. At the word of Jesus, the need is met, and the wine he provides is far better than the best the host had to offer (vs. 9-10). The true joy that God's people will know fully in the age to come is to be found in faithful acceptance of what Jesus provides.

The story of the cleansing of the Temple at Jerusalem (ch. 2:13-22) is a prime example of John's fondness for multiple meanings. The words of the Gospel narrative itself show that the Temple is a symbol for the body of Jesus, which is to be raised up "in three days." But John also shows that the destruction of the Temple signifies the inadequacy of the Jewish mode of worship. A third meaning, however, appears in this story: it is a prophecy of the establishment of the new Temple, which is the body of Christ (the church). That new body can come into being only after the body of Jesus has been broken in death and raised to new life.

The symbolic meaning of the story of the feeding of five thousand is given quite explicitly (John 6:25-65). The kind of satisfaction that men work to gain ends in frustration and emptiness, but the sense of gratification and fulfillment that Christ makes possible not only sustains life as it is now known but "endures to eternal life" (v. 27). Although the ultimate reference of Jesus' words about bread is to spiritual sustenance, there seems to be also a secondary meaning in which the sacrament of the Lord's Supper is meant. The word for "giving thanks" (v. 11) is the source of our word "Eucharist," the sacrament of the Lord's Supper. To speak of eating the flesh and drinking the blood of the Son of God (v. 53) are figurative ways of describing the intimate fellowship that God's people have with Jesus Christ through common participation in the Sacrament. But in order to stress the fact that the physical substances of the Sacrament do not convey spiritual life automatically, Jesus says, "It is the spirit that gives life, the flesh [i.e., the bread and wine in themselves] is of no avail" (v. 63).

In the story of the healing of the paralytic, the emphasis placed on the man's complete helplessness is symbolic. The old way of life cannot provide health and wholeness. There is irony in the fact that the healing took place on the Sabbath, the day that attested the completion of God's work in creating the world (Gen. 2:1-2) and that prefigured the coming day of rest when all God's purposes for his creation would be fulfilled.

Instead of seeing that this man's being healed on the Sabbath was a foretaste of the final defeat of sickness and evil, the Jews are incensed because it violates their law. (By "the Jews," John means the Jewish officials, especially the leaders of the priests and the ruling class, not the Jews in general.) The paralytic's being healed is an anticipation of that day when all those who now are helpless under legalistic religion, or who simply hope something will happen (John 5:7), will find strength and release in Jesus Christ.

The officer whose son was healed by Jesus in the story told by John (ch. 4:46-54) was probably a Gentile, so that his faith is all the more remarkable, contrasting as it does with the unbelief of official Jewry. The theme of God's invitation to all who will respond is first encountered in ch. 1:11-12, where the writer states that, having been rejected by his own people, Jesus Christ extends the opportunity of membership in the people of God to all who will respond in faith to his word. Step by step as the Gospel proceeds, the writer shows how Jewish opposition mounts. Popular support flares up when Jesus has fed the people, and they want to make him king (ch. 6:15). But his rejection of their kind of kingship dissolves their esteem into deep hostility (ch. 8:59).

But he invites all who will to become a part of his flock (ch. 10:16). The figure of the flock is a mixed metaphor: Jesus is both the shepherd (v. 11) and the door into the sheepfold (v. 7). Those who enter the fold are those who hear and heed his voice (v. 16). They correspond to the persons referred to in ch. 1:12: "To all who received him, . . . he gave power to become children of God." When Jesus hears that a group of Greeks have come, he knows that the hour is at hand for the completion of his mission (ch. 12:20-24). Access into the fellowship of God's people is open to all who will receive him as God's final Word to man.

The conviction that the Jewish officials are blind to God's truth is vividly portrayed in ch. 9, in the story of the man born blind. They are concerned only for the argument about sin and sickness: first, whether the man was blind because he or his parents had sinned; second, whether a man who broke the Sabbath as Jesus did could really heal anyone. The man born blind is not interested in theological causes, or in the consequences of breaking religious rules, or in the qualifications of Jesus. All that concerns him is that once he was blind, and now he can see (v. 25). Because he takes this stand of unquestioning gratitude toward Jesus, he is put out of the synagogue, and, by implication, out of the fellowship of those who think they are God's own people. But the man demonstrates in his conversation with Jesus that he is already a part of the true people of faith (v. 38). Those who quarreled about the causes of blindness and the consequences of sin are the ones who are blind (vs. 30, 41).

The resurrection of Lazarus epitomizes Jewish piety. His sisters, Mary and Martha, enjoy the close-knit fellowship of the home; they grieve at the passing of a member of the family; they look forward to the distant and unpredictable day of resurrection and judgment when all men will stand before God. They believe that Jesus might have been able to restore their ailing brother to health, but now that he has died, there remains only the traditional hope for vindication in the Last Day. But the life that Jesus brings to man is far more than a mere restoration of the old life; it is an entirely new order of life. In him, eternal life begins now, and the promise of life beyond death already begins to be fulfilled. He does more than bring a message about this new life; he is himself the embodiment of it (ch. 11:25). Once more, the reaction of the Jewish leaders to this sign is hostile fear that somehow this unprecedented power may undermine their own authority or threaten their favored place. "So from that day on they took counsel how to put [Jesus] to death." (Ch. 11:53.)

"I Am He"

After the incident of the feeding of the five thousand, Jesus is in controversy with "the Jews" over his authority. He claims that his word takes precedence over Abraham (ch. 8:51-58). In response to their challenge of his statements, Jesus declares: "Before Abraham was, I am." The Greek phrase translated "I am" is in turn a translation of the Old Testament Hebrew expression in which God declares his eternal existence, unchanged by the shifting face of history and of human affairs:

> "Turn to me and be saved,
>   all the ends of the earth!
>   For I am God, and there is no other."
>
> (Isa. 45:22.)

John identifies Jesus with God and his eternal purpose by putting on his lips the strange yet eloquent phrase, "I am." John has prepared the way for this bold affirmation by mention in ch. 8:23 of Jesus' heavenly origin. The Jewish leadership has its origin among men. Jesus and his mission have their origin with God, so that neither he nor his mission can be said to have begun merely with the appearance in Galilee of Jesus of Nazareth. In him, indeed, the Word of God has been made flesh. (Ch. 1:14.)

The phrase "I am" is used by John to unfold the full meaning of God's purpose as it is disclosed in his Messiah. The first significant occurrence of this phrase is at ch. 6:35, where Jesus says: "I am the bread of life." Unlike ordinary bread, he is able to sustain life for eternity, and to provide new fullness and richness of life that is not otherwise available to man. The bread is not only something Jesus Christ provides: he *is* that bread. Similarly, in ch. 8:1, Jesus *is* the Light of the World. He embodies in himself the light of the knowledge of God and his purposes for man. The same intention lies behind the statements in chs. 11:25 and 14:6, where Jesus says he is "the resurrection and the life," "the way, and the truth, and the life." These are qualities that are actualized in the life of a historical person, not merely abstract ideas or religious teachings. The faith that John seeks to evoke from his hearers is not assent to Jesus' religious views, but response to Jesus *himself*.

A second group of "I am" sayings discloses the relationship between Jesus Christ and the people of God. Jesus is "the door" by which men enter into the common life of God's flock (ch. 10:7). He is "the good shepherd" who cares for his people, protecting them from attackers and supplying their common needs (v. 11). He is "the true vine," through which the common life of believers is sustained and by which the fruitfulness of Christian living is made possible (ch. 15:1).

"I AND THE FATHER ARE ONE"

The Gospel of John affirms in the strongest terms both (1) the human origins and limitations of Jesus and (2) his oneness with God the Father. Instead of setting Jesus apart from other human beings by the belief in the virgin birth, John states flatly that Jesus was the son of Joseph (ch. 1:45) and infers that he was born in Galilee rather than Bethlehem (ch. 7:41-42). Throughout the book, stress is laid on his human qualities — fatigue, thirst, sorrow — and on the fact that his body in the resurrection was visible and tangible (ch. 20:24-28). The paradox is sharpest when Thomas, realizing at last that he can put his hand into the side of Christ's body, utters the most thoroughgoing statement of Jesus' divinity: "My Lord and my God!"

John says unequivocally that the Word of God, which was

made flesh in Jesus of Nazareth, has coexisted with God from
eternity (ch. 1:1). He is careful to point out that God and the
Word are not interchangeable terms. Rather, the Word pos-
sesses the essential qualities of God, just as I John 4:8 says that
love is the essential quality of God. The presence and activity
of the Word in Jesus Christ places him in a unique relationship, so that he is called *the* Son, and as such is the agent
through whom the glory of God is manifested (John 1:18).
He is still Jesus of Nazareth, the son of Joseph (v. 45), although he is also the Son and the King of God's people (v. 49).

But wherein lies the unity of the Father and the Son? It is
by no means a matter of simple identity, as though Jesus was
God the Father in disguise. The Son utters the words of God
(ch. 3:34); he does what he sees the Father doing (ch. 5:19).
Because he claims to be working God's works in his healing
ministry, "the Jews" accuse him of making himself equal
with God (v. 18). The Father has committed all judgment to
the Son, and has given him the power to give life (vs. 21-22).
The Son is the supreme object of the Father's love, and honor
and obedience to the Son are tantamount to honor and obedience to the Father. The Son comes in the authority of the
Father (v. 43) and his works bear witness that the Father has
sent him (v. 36). What the Son declares to the world is what
he has heard from God (ch. 8:37, 40). He does only what is
pleasing in the Father's sight (v. 29). The Son came from God,
because he was sent by God (v. 42). When, at the end of ch. 10,
the Jewish leaders finally denounce Jesus as a blasphemer, it
is in reaction to his claim that the works he has been doing
are God's works. This claim is interpreted by his hearers as
equivalent to making himself God (v. 33). But the oneness of
Jesus with God is a unity of works, of will, of devotion, of
obedience by which Jesus is uniquely the instrument of God's
purpose to disclose his nature and create his people.

"That They May All Be One"

Another unity for which John is concerned is the unity of the people of God. The people of God bear the same relationship to Jesus Christ that he bears to God the Father. As God sent Christ, so Christ sends forth his people (ch. 17:18). As the Father gave his word to the Son, so the Son gives God's words to his people (vs. 8, 14). The glory that God gave to Jesus Christ he has given to them; the love with which God loved him he has poured out upon them (vs. 22-23). The Son went forth in the Father's name; they are to go forth in the confidence that if they ask the Father anything in the Son's name, their petition will be heard (ch. 15:16). They are to bear witness to Christ as he bore witness to God (vs. 26-27). Most surprising of all, just as Jesus did his works because of God at work through him, so Jesus' people will do the same, and even greater, works (ch. 14:11-12). The Word of God, which was made flesh in Jesus Christ, is still at work through God's new people. And it will continue to work until all God's people are united (ch. 17:23).

It would be a mistake, however, to suppose that the church is for John nothing more than an extension of Jesus Christ. Just as the Word made flesh is distinct from God himself, so Christ's people are distinct from him. But there is one eternal purpose that flows from God through Christ to and through his people. John identifies this ongoing activity of God in the world through his people as the Spirit. He continues the testimony to Christ (ch. 15:26), guides God's people into the truth (ch. 16:13), glorifies Christ as Christ glorified God the Father (v. 14). He is sent by the Son, just as the Son was sent by the Father (v. 7). His work is to sustain the life that God gave his people through the Son (ch. 7:38-39).

Significantly, it is when the disciples are gathered on the first day of the week — the time when Christians unite for worship, for fellowship, for mutual strengthening — that the risen Lord appears and gives them the Spirit. With the gift of the Spirit goes authority to pronounce the word of forgiveness (ch. 20:23). With the Spirit comes the gift of peace (v. 21).

After the Spirit had been given, the disciples were challenged to unite together in order to carry out their mission (ch. 21:1-19). In the midst of their summons to serve, they met with their Lord in a common meal of bread and fish (vs. 12-14; fish is a very ancient symbol of the Lord's Supper). But their mission was not only to draw in those who might become God's people, but to nurture those who already were his children. Hence the repeated command: " Feed my lambs . . . feed my sheep " (vs. 15-17). Only by fulfilling the commission can God's people demonstrate their love. Only as they are willing to obey his command, even when it demands that they give up their lives, can they be ready to heed the call: " Follow me." Nothing less than this is worthy of those who call themselves by the name of Jesus Christ, and take their place among the new people of God.